Trade What You See

Founded in 1807, John Wiley & Sons is the oldest independent publishing company in the United States. With offices in North America, Europe, Australia and Asia, Wiley is globally committed to developing and marketing print and electronic products and services for our customers' professional and personal knowledge and understanding.

The Wiley Trading series features books by traders who have survived the market's ever-changing temperament and have prosperedsome by reinventing systems, others by getting back to basics. Whether a novice trader, professional or somewhere in between, these books will provide the advice and strategies needed to prosper today and well into the future.

For a list of available titles, please visit our Web site at www.WileyFinance.com.

Trade What You See

How to Profit from Pattern Recognition

LARRY PESAVENTO
LESLIE JOUFLAS

John Wiley & Sons, Inc.

Published by John Wiley & Sons, Inc., Hoboken, New Jersey
Published simultaneously in Canada.

Wiley Bicentennial Logo: Richard J. Pacifico

For general information on our other products and services or for technical support, please contact our Customer Care Department within the United States at (800) 762-2974, outside the United States at (317) 572-3993 or fax (317) 572-4002.

Wiley also publishes its books in a variety of electronic formats. Some content that appears in print may not be available in electronic books. For more information about Wiley products, visit our web site at www.wiley.com.

Library of Congress Cataloging-in-Publication Data:

Pesavento, Larry.
  Trade what you see : how to profit from pattern recognition / Larry
Pesavento, Leslie Jouflas.
      p.   cm. – (Wiley trading series)
  Includes index.
  ISBN 978-0-470-10676-1 (cloth)
 1. Speculation. 2. Stocks. 3. Investment analysis. 4. Fibonacci numbers.
I. Jouflas, Leslie, 1957– II. Title.
  HG6041.P382 2008
  332.63′228–dc22

                                                            2007034476

Printed in the United States of America

10 9 8 7 6 5 4 3

To all traders, past and present, who have dedicated themselves to becoming successful at making a living in the profession of trading.

Contents

Preface   xi

Acknowledgments   xv

About the Authors   xvii

PART I   Introduction to Trading with Pattern Recognition

CHAPTER 1   Opening Thoughts   3

How to Use This Book   3
Succeeding or Failing in Trading   4
Steps to Take for Successful Trading   7

CHAPTER 2   Geometry of the Patterns and Fibonacci Ratios   9

History of Geometry in the Markets   11
Fibonacci Ratios   13
Applying the Fibonacci Ratios   15
Summary   18

CHAPTER 3   Harmonic Numbers and How to Use Them   19

Where the Term *Harmonic Numbers* Originated   19
Defining a Harmonic Number   20
Vibrations in Price Swings   22
Repetition in Price Swings   24
Finding Harmonic Numbers   28
Harmonic Numbers Found in Other Markets   34

PART II   The Price Patterns and How to Trade Them

CHAPTER 4   The AB=CD Pattern   **37**

History of the AB=CD Pattern   37
AB=CD Pattern Description   39
AB=CD Pattern Structure   39
Important Characteristics of the AB=CD Pattern   42
CD Leg Variations   43
Slope and Time Frames   46
Psychology of the AB=CD Pattern   48
Trading the AB=CD Pattern   49

CHAPTER 5   The Gartley "222" Pattern   **53**

History of the Gartley "222" Pattern   53
Gartley "222" Pattern Description   55
Gartley "222" Pattern Structure   56
Important Characteristics of the Gartley "222" Pattern   57
Psychology of the Gartley "222" Pattern   59
Trading the Gartley "222" Pattern   60

CHAPTER 6   The Butterfly Pattern   **67**

History of the Butterfly Pattern   67
Butterfly Pattern Description   69
Butterfly Pattern Structure   70
Important Characteristics of the Butterfly Pattern   71
Psychology of the Butterfly Pattern   72
Trading the Butterfly Pattern   73

CHAPTER 7   The Three Drives Pattern   **81**

History of the Three Drives Pattern   81
Three Drives Pattern Description   82
Three Drives Pattern Structure   83
Important Characteristics of the Three Drives Pattern   84
Psychology of the Three Drives Pattern   84
Trading the Three Drives Pattern   85

CHAPTER 8   Retracement Entries and Multiple Time Frames   **91**

Fibonacci Retracement Entries   92
Fibonacci Retracement Pattern Structure   92
Trading the Fibonacci Retracement Pattern   95
Opening Price Retracement Setups   98
Market Setup for the Opening Price Retracement Trade   99
Trading the Opening Price Retracement Setup   100
Multiple Time Frames   103

CHAPTER 9   Classical Technical Analysis Patterns   **113**

A Brief History of Technical Analysis   114
Basics of Technical Analysis   115
Double Bottom and Top Patterns   115
Head and Shoulders Pattern   120
Broadening Top and Bottom Patterns   126

CHAPTER 10   Learning to Recognize Trend Days   **131**

Identifying a Trend Day   132
Patterns Found on Trend Days   135
Fibonacci Ratios on Trend Days   138
Controlling Risk on a Trend Day   140
Trading a Trend Day   141

PART III   Essential Elements of Trading

CHAPTER 11   Trade Management   **149**

Thinking in Probabilities   150
Warning Signs and Confirmation Signs   151
Money Management   155

**CHAPTER 12   Using Options with the Fibonacci
                Ratios and Patterns**   **161**

Call and Put Options Defined   161
Factors That Influence the Price of an Option   162

Controlling Risk with Options   163
Examples of Using Options with Extension Patterns   164

CHAPTER 13   Building a Trading Plan   **167**

Daily Trading Plan   168
Trading as a Business   174
Disaster Plans   177
Summary   181

CHAPTER 14   Daily Routines   **183**

Trade Preparation   183
Mental Preparation   187
Physical Preparation   188

Appendix   **191**

Index   **195**

Preface

"Trading is a journey—not a destination."

Several hundred years ago, technical analysis began its journey to help investors and traders determine, with reasonable probability, what direction prices might take. Technical analysis allows investors and traders to identify moments of opportunity to profit in the markets. It does so by identifying and quantifying specific patterns that form and repeat with enough regularity that trading methods and strategies can be developed and implemented with success.

Trade What You See: How to Profit from Pattern Recognition focuses on trading patterns with an underlying root structure based on simple geometric forms and Fibonacci ratios. The patterns are easily identifiable once the trader has spent some time observing and learning the basic structures. Each of these patterns can be quantified and a sound money management strategy applied.

Writing a book about pattern recognition based on geometric patterns and Fibonacci ratios requires acknowledging the early scholars of geometry, including Pythagoras, Archimedes, and of course the great mathematician Leonardo di Pisa (better known as Fibonacci). These great scholars had all traveled to Egypt during their lifetimes and had studied the Great Pyramids. Pythagoras, the father of modern geometry, was obsessed by the mathematics of the pyramids. The actual mass of the structure was not as important to him as the fact that all of the angles on all sides were within .01 percent. Part of the mystery of the Great Pyramids is how the mathematics relates to the golden ratio, which is also referred to as the divine proportion, or .618.

It was not so many years ago that a book of this nature, based on technical analysis, would not have been taken seriously by many. We begin with a look at a point in time when technical analysis had begun to take root in the academic community.

VALIDATION FROM THE SCIENTIFIC COMMUNITY

For years technical analysis was shunned by many Wall Street professionals, looked upon as one step above tea leaf reading. A turning point occurred on April 17, 2000, when a paper by Dr. Andrew W. Lo of the Massachusetts Institute of Technology (MIT) was published in *BusinessWeek*. The title of the article was "This Alchemy Will Yield Pure Gold." The article substantiated and verified that indeed there is an edge in technical analysis after all. This, of course, did not surprise any market technician who had successfully been using pattern recognition.

The article did, however, bring technical analysis from the age of alchemy into the realm of academia. Princeton University Press published a book by Dr. Lo and A. Craig MacKinlay, *A Non-Random Walk Down Wall Street*, which analyzed why patterns work and how they repeat. This could be one of the reasons that the financial public is now exposed to so many chart patterns in the financial press and on television.

Long before Lo and MacKinlay's book was published, there were many great technical analysts to whom today we owe a debt of gratitude. Some of these technical analysts who have contributed groundbreaking work are H.M. Gartley, William Garrett, Edwards and McGhee, Frank Tubbs, R.W. Schabacker, William Dunnigan, Ralph Elliott, John Murphy, Linda Raschke, John Hill, Bryce Gilmore, Charles Lindsay, and Richard Wyckoff. We regret if we unintentionally omitted any famous names.

What this book teaches is a simple, pragmatic approach to pattern recognition. It's designed to be hands-on and to appeal to new students of technical analysis as well as seasoned traders.

The motto that we trade by is "Trade what you see, not what you believe." A true technician is interested only in price bars and the summation of these price bars—the only truth in trading. Traders must learn to believe in what the market is telling them based on price. This is best accomplished by studying price behavior through pattern recognition.

OVERVIEW OF THE BOOK

This book was written to give the reader a comprehensive view of the specific patterns presented. We use a variety of stocks and markets in the chart examples throughout the book to illustrate that these particular patterns do form in all markets, and in all time frames. We present patterns derived from some of the classic technical analysis patterns as well as the geometry and Fibonacci-based patterns. Here is an overview of each chapter:

Chapter 1: Opening Thoughts—We give the reader some of our observations on what is needed to successfully use the information in this book. We also offer our insights after dealing with hundreds of traders on what can make a successful trader and also what leads to failure.

Chapter 2: Geometry of the Markets and Fibonacci Ratios—This chapter covers the simple geometry of the markets and how the x-axis and y-axis provide just another way of illustrating triangles. We also cover the history of Fibonacci ratios and present the ones we apply to our trading.

Chapter 3: Harmonic Numbers and How to Use Them—This chapter shows that all financial markets have what we refer to as harmonic and repetitive swings that are inherent in each particular market. This chapter begins to outline the basic structure of each pattern.

Chapter 4: The AB=CD Pattern—The AB=CD pattern is one of the simplest to identify in any market, on any time frame, and is the basis of several other patterns presented.

Chapter 5: The Gartley "222" Pattern—Derived from Gartley's work in the 1930s, this pattern is a classic retracement pattern.

Chapter 6: The Butterfly Pattern—The Butterfly pattern is seen at extreme turning points in tops and bottoms; it is ideal for options trades and allows low-risk entries.

Chapter 7: Three Drives Pattern—This pattern can signal either a major turning point or a more complex correction in a trend. It is very easy to see on a price chart when it forms.

Chapter 8: Retracement Entries and Multiple Time Frames—We cover simple retracement patterns with Fibonacci ratios that we use to enter in the direction of a trend. We also look at how to combine multiple time frames.

Chapter 9: Classical Technical Analysis Patterns—Patterns such as Head and Shoulders, Double Tops and Bottoms, and Broadening Tops and Bottoms are discussed using Fibonacci ratios.

Chapter 10: Learning to Recognize Trend Days—This chapter could pay for the book many times over. It teaches traders how to identify trending conditions and offers techniques for entering in the direction of the trend. We also show how to use Fibonacci ratios as support and resistance in trends. We emphasize the importance of staying out of countertrend trades when a strong trend is in progress.

Chapter 11: Trade Management—The secret to trade management is in understanding that risk is the most important element in trading. We look at position sizes and methods for determining total risk. This chapter covers which warning signs we use and the confirmation signals for trade entry or for passing on a trade altogether.

Chapter 12: Using Options with the Fibonacci Ratios and Patterns—Options are available on nearly every liquid trading vehicle. Pattern recognition, because it is a leading indicator, is applicable to options. We present some basic option strategies that minimize risk and allow for substantial profits.

Chapter 13: Building a Trading Plan—Once readers have studied the patterns, they can then move on to a trading plan. This chapter gives a solid foundation to build a plan that can be expanded upon as the trader gains experience. Over half a century of trading experience was used to describe the formulation of a trading plan.

Chapter 14: Daily Routines—Routines and rituals are a necessary part of the trading profession. The difference between successful traders and unsuccessful traders is in the thought process and the preparation. The successful trader does the same things every day to prepare for trading. This chapter gives suggestions for daily routines.

The appendix includes our lists of recommended books, magazines, and web site resources.

As a trader using pattern recognition, it is your job to learn these repetitive patterns and discover the underlying price ratios that lead to a predictive nature. We hope that you find this book a valuable guide and reference as you progress. We wish you a long and prosperous trading journey.

Acknowledgments

We would like to thank Robin Farina and Rich Crane for their patience, time, and outstanding help with this book. We also would like to thank our friends John Arrington and Howard Arrington at Ensign Software; all the chart examples in this book were generated from their software, which is user friendly to our methodology. We'd like to thank Shelli Simon for her efforts and time. Thanks to John Hill from *Futures Truth* for his willingness to share some of the information obtained and some of the rare books mentioned. Thank you to Mark Douglas and Linda Raschke for their reviews and comments. Thanks to Jon and Liz Maresca for their support in everything.

Special thanks to Gary Porter, who patiently read each word and chapter as though he were a student of this methodology. His comments and insights are greatly appreciated.

A grateful thank-you to all those at John Wiley & Sons, Inc., who gave us the opportunity to write this book. Thank you, Emilie Herman, for all of your time—it is greatly appreciated.

It would be impossible to list all the great masters who have since passed on to that big trading room, but some of the more important ones to us do have their names mentioned in the book, as well as the ones still with us. The contributions of those mentioned in this book cannot be underestimated in the development of technical analysis of speculative markets.

SPECIAL THANKS AND ACKNOWLEDGMENT

I would like to give special thanks and gratitude to Larry Pesavento. You introduced me to seeing the fascinating, harmonic world of Fibonacci ratios in the markets. Thank you for inspiring me and helping me develop my enthusiasm into a solid trading methodology. Thank you for starting me on that journey.

I am especially thankful to my family—my Mom and Dad, my brothers Marty and Todd—for their support throughout my trading career. I am especially grateful to Gary, my husband, for his never-ending support.

Leslie Jouflas

About the Authors

Larry Pesavento is registered with the Commodity Futures Trading Commission, National Futures Association, and Securities and Exchange Commission, and is a former member of the Chicago Mercantile Exchange (1981–1983). He has a BS in Pharmaceutical Chemistry (Indiana State University, 1963) and an MBA in Finance from Indiana State University (1970). Books he has written on the subject of trading include: *Astro-cycles: The Traders Viewpoint* (Traders Press, 1987); *Planetary Harmonics for Speculative Markets* (Traders Press, 1990); *Harmonic Vibrations: A Metamorphosis from Traditional Cycle Theory to Astro-Harmonics* (Traders Press, 1990); *Fibonacci Ratios with Pattern Recognition* (Traders Press, 1997); *Profitable Patterns for Stock Trading* (Traders Press, 1999); *The Opening Price Principle*, with Peggy MacKay (Traders Press, 2000); *Private Thoughts from a Trader's Diary*, with Peggy MacKay (Traders Press, 2002); *Essentials of Trading: It's Not WHAT You Think, It's HOW You Think*, with Leslie Jouflas (Traders Press, 2006). Larry can be contacted at larry@tradingtutor.com.

Leslie Jouflas began trading in 1996 and left a 17-year airline career in 2000 to pursue a full-time trading career. She has studied many trading methodologies, including Elliott Wave, options strategies, momentum trading, classical technical analysis, and Fibonacci ratios and patterns. After trading stocks and options on stocks, she now trades futures and commodities with an emphasis on the S&P 500 market. She manages private accounts as well as trading her own private account. Leslie has written several articles for such publications as *Trader's Journal*, *Active Trader*, and *Technical Analysis of Stocks & Commodities*. She co-authored *Essentials of Trading: It's Not WHAT You Think, It's HOW You Think* (Traders Press, 2006). Leslie teaches workshops and is available for speaking engagements. She also coaches and tutors students in pattern recognition trading with an emphasis on improving and refining execution skills. Leslie can be contacted at ljouflas@msn.com or at www.tradingliveonline.com.

PART I

Introduction to Trading with Pattern Recognition

CHAPTER 1

Opening
Thoughts

We have had the opportunity to come in contact with many traders over the years. Some are just entering this field, while others are experienced, successful traders. We thought it would be helpful to the reader of this book to hear our comments and observations on why some traders succeed and why some fail at trading.

As you read this book and study the methodology, we hope these insights will help to keep you on a path to success in trading. Trading requires hard work and perseverance. At times it can be a process of two steps forward and three steps back. Once you do find a consistent successful approach, though, there is nothing like the business of trading.

In this first chapter we cover what is the best way to use this book. We give our thoughts on why traders succeed or fail in trading, and offer suggestions for actions traders can take for successful trading.

HOW TO USE THIS BOOK

You will see as you progress through this book, we present many specific chart patterns and include suggestions for how to enter and manage those setups. We would suggest you start by keeping it simple and study a couple of patterns each day.

We also suggest that you work through the patterns in the order they're presented. Start with the basics—geometry (Chapter 2) and harmonics (Chapter 3)—before moving on to the pattern formations. This will help you build a solid foundation and understanding of what we are teaching.

We include many examples of trades in each pattern chapter. Once you have a basic foundation in place of the pattern structures, you will be ready to study how these patterns are traded, and begin to think in terms of implementing these into your trading. We always recommend traders do some form of paper trading or simulated trading before committing real funds.

Learning how markets work is accomplished through time and experience. This is invaluable to the trader or investor. Determining what type of trading environment one is in, such as a trend environment versus a range environment, is important. Recognizing the subtle symmetry in all markets is an absolute prerequisite for a pattern recognition trader; this is done only one way: practice, practice, and more practice.

The only way the information in this book can be used to make money is to understand each pattern and apply sound trading principles. To help each trader accomplish this, we offer guidelines on developing a trading plan, covering pattern recognition, thinking in terms of probabilities, money management, risk assessment, and techniques for entering and exiting trades. Other subjects include setting up trading as a business and preparing for the unexpected. Treating trading as anything other than a business is a mistake. Even if the trader is not trading full-time, trading activities should be treated and set up as a second business.

A note on some of the charts throughout the book: Many of the chart examples are of the S&P 500 E-mini contract. This is an extremely popular market for traders and very conducive to the patterns presented in this book. You will find some of these charts labeled as "ES," which is the root symbol for the S&P 500; others are labeled as S&P 500.

SUCCEEDING OR FAILING IN TRADING

It is each trader's responsibility to develop the skills and discipline necessary for successful trading. We have not found and do not know of a holy grail in trading or an easy trading method. In many classic trading books, like *Profits in the Stock Market*, by H.M. Gartley (1935), there are observations about what accounts for successful versus unsuccessful trading. Interestingly, we have not seen many changes over the decades in this area. It seems to be the same aspects that constantly plague traders. There are, however, many actions the individual trader can implement to succeed.

Trading is like any other profession; the student first learns the basics, and then expands to more sophisticated and in-depth learning in the chosen field. There are no skilled professionals in any field who have not reached a level of expertise without hard work and substantial experience. Any professional field requires a commitment and willingness to go through successes as well as failures. The failures can be the greatest teachers. Study the failures to develop into a better trader. Perseverance will be a key to a successful trading career.

Developing a mind-set that is conducive to trading will be essential to a trader's success. This will include thinking in terms of probabilities, and accepting the fact that losses are as much a part of trading as wins. This is a process in itself to learn. These concepts must be internalized so they become a part of what you do each day without conscious thought.

Larry Schneider, director of business developments for the Zaner Group, futures and commodities brokers, states that often too much time is focused on learning the method or system in the beginning. This approach is contrary to the steps that must be done to meet success in trading. In his view and experience, focusing on learning a mental approach first would be more beneficial to novice traders. He says it is imperative for traders to understand that there is a learning curve and money can be lost if traders do not take steps to protect their capital.

Every trader has to go through essentially the same learning curve; no one seems to be exempt from it. Schneider suggests, from his experience of 34 years in the futures business, that traders start small, perhaps with the mini contracts available, while they are learning. If traders take the time to investigate the mental approach they will need to execute their plan, they will be far ahead of the game. His advice is to approach trading from the mental side first, *then* develop your trading methodology and plan.

Why Traders Succeed

We work with, coach, and mentor many traders. We see and have experienced the full gamut of things that can happen in trading. Here are some of the reasons we feel traders succeed:

- Solid knowledge and understanding of the markets they are trading.
- Technical expertise on how to trade their markets.
- A sound trading methodology with a proven edge.
- A trading plan based on the methodology.
- Sufficient capital.
- Thinking in terms of probabilities, rather than emphasis on the outcome of any one trade.
- Good money management; adherence to money management rules.
- Having mentors or seeking out experts and peers to gain trading knowledge.
- Assessing risk first, profits second.

- Employment of a set of trading rules.
- A foundation of daily routines, including mental preparation.
- Use of stop-loss protection.
- Maintenance of a high level of confidence and a positive attitude.
- Commitment to the process of trading.
- Perseverance.
- Taking 100 percent responsibility for each and everything that happens in their trading.
- Being in the habit of forgetting their last trade, win or lose, and moving on to the next trade.

Why Traders Fail

Conversely, we also see particular reasons traders fail. We would like to share these observations with you in the hope you can learn from these errors and avoid some of these pitfalls. An ancient proverb states, "The smart man learns from his mistakes—the wise man learns from the mistakes of others."

- Lack of knowledge; traders enter the business constantly without a solid understanding of what the business of speculation involves.
- Lack of capital; small accounts typically lose money. Those few with smaller accounts who do succeed eventually hang on until they understand how leverage can be friend or foe.
- No trading methodology; they use a seat-of-the-pants approach.
- No trading plan.
- Failure to apply a solid money management system.
- Not seeking help from experts or mentors; not wanting to invest in an education of trading.
- Lack of understanding of the inherent risks present in trading.
- Failure to recognize the mental preparation necessary for successful trading.
- No trading rules applied.
- Altering a sound trading plan; early entries, early exits, moving stops, not entering trade setups.
- Random trading, which is trading anything outside of their trading plan and is usually emotion-based.
- Failure to develop the discipline necessary to trade successfully.
- Not learning from previous mistakes.
- Lack of commitment to the process of trading.

- Failure to use stop-loss orders, which is the number one way to turn a small loss into a large loss.
- Blaming outcomes on external sources and not taking 100 percent responsibility for each and every aspect of their trading.

STEPS TO TAKE FOR SUCCESSFUL TRADING

One very important item to keep in mind while learning to trade: *Each action you take repeatedly will become a habit.* The habits that form will lead to either your success or your failure. Habits in and of themselves are neutral; they do not know if they have a positive or negative effect. However, the results of the habits will have a negative or positive outcome in your trading. Therefore, it is in the best interest of each trader to strive to form the very best habits that will ensure success.

Traders want to strive for a point in their trading where they are just doing the necessary actions. They should have a high confidence level that over time the edge in their trading will have a positive expectation. This will be developed through testing and implementing a specific trading strategy. We hope the items we have listed will help you determine which direction you are taking.

If you are an experienced trader and you have already formed habits that are not producing the desired results, then take time to evaluate your trading and begin to form new habits that will get you the results you desire in trading. Chapter 13 has a worksheet titled "Twenty Sample Trades Worksheet" (Figure 13.2), designed to help traders instill new trading habits. It focuses on doing the same positive action through a series of trades to create new habits and to observe how the trading edge is played out.

Positive habits will produce positive results. Negative habits will produce negative results and will be self-defeating. It may be helpful to make a list of any negative habits that are present in your trading, and a separate list of positive habits to replace those.

An example of a negative habit may be that the trader consistently exits a trade before the profit objective is reached. The new positive habit will have the trader hold for the profit objective. Another example may be that the trader enters early before a pattern is completed. The new positive habit will have the trader enter at the correct entry point. Once traders understand and know what their edge is, they will begin to see the importance of consistently executing their plan. They will see if there is a gap between where they are and where they want to be. This is a point where the trader can then fill in the necessary steps to close that gap.

Conversely, pay attention to your positive habits. The actions you are doing right in your trading can be developed further into strengths.

Develop support systems to help you instill new positive habits. A support system may be using a buddy system with another trader. It never hurts to have accountability with someone else that can help keep you on the path to your goals, but in the long run each action is your responsibility.

Here is a list you can use to help develop your personal plan of action to reach the success level you want in trading:

- Create positive habits.
- Replace negative habits with positive habits.
- Take 100 percent responsibility for each outcome.
- Create a support system to help keep you on the path to your goals.
- Take a proactive approach to making changes in your trading.

Start with a list of actions that you need to take to reach your goals. Believe in yourself; know that you are a successful trader.

As you study the trading patterns in this book, we hope that the aforementioned items will help you to develop as a successful trader.

CHAPTER 2

Geometry of the Patterns and Fibonacci Ratios

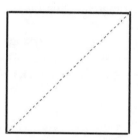

Ａll of the patterns presented in this book are based in geometry; the structure of each pattern is geometrical. As we go through each pattern chapter, we discuss and present the structure of each pattern so that you will learn and understand how each pattern is formed. First, though, this chapter gives an overview and brief history of geometry in the markets. We hope to impart to you the importance that geometry plays in the markets and especially in the patterns presented in this book.

We will give you a glimpse into the studies of some of the market forefathers who pioneered this aspect of market study, such as W.D. Gann, George Bayer, and Bryce Gilmore, author of *The Geometry of Markets*.

Figure 2.1 gives a clear idea of what we are referring to throughout the book when we mention a geometric triangle or symmetrical pattern. It shows a perfect triangle that was formed by price, creating a trading opportunity.

Figure 2.2, in contrast, shows an asymmetrical geometric pattern, and generally we want to filter out those patterns and look for the ones with the best symmetry. This example shows an extreme expansion in this market that was trending. Note the long

FIGURE 2.1   Example of symmetrical triangle shape formed by price.

range bars signifying a wide price range for the time period; this is a warning sign and is discussed in detail in Chapter 11.

One more example shows two symmetrical triangles, refer to Figure 2.3 which are the basis for the AB=CD pattern (covered in Chapter 4). Repeatedly throughout the book we stress symmetry, and after you study the patterns, you will come away with a good understanding of this principle.

FIGURE 2.2   Example of asymmetrical triangle.

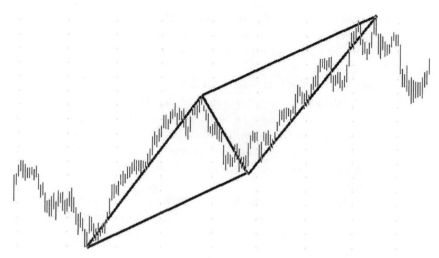

FIGURE 2.3 Example of two symmetrical triangles forming an AB=CD pattern.

HISTORY OF GEOMETRY IN THE MARKETS

The history of technical analysis and its relationship to geometry began in the 1930s with the work of W.D. Gann. Gann became famous for the use of Gann angles, which are now found in many charting software packages. These angles were especially well known for the 45-degree line and his square of 9 charts, which basically divided a circle into 12 30-degree sections. In fact, this was a way of using harmonic numbers (see Chapter 3 on harmonic numbers), but was arrived at very differently than how we discuss them in this book.

There was always much speculation around Gann's life and work after his death in the early 1950s. There are stories that he made more than $55 million trading, although his surviving four children attested that this was not the case and that his estate had been worth around $250,000, which in the 1950s was still a considerable amount.

In the 1930s, a trader by the name of George Bayer introduced the total Fibonacci summation series to traders. He wrote several books; one in particular, called *The Egg of Columbus*, was once offered for sale in the mid-1980s for $25,000. Extremely rare and less than 100 pages long, the book was difficult for most readers to understand. In it Bayer described the progression of the Fibonacci series using diagrams of birds, fish, and mammals as a type of mystical code. The code was apparent to those familiar with the Fibonacci summation series but very difficult for anyone not familiar with it. He may have been trying to alert his readers to the strong numerical ties that linked Fibonacci numbers and astronomy.

Unlike Gann's children, Bayer's daughter stated that her father had made a very successful living from the business of speculation. Each year he would take his private rail car from his home in Carmel, California, and travel to the Chicago Board of Trade to trade the grains.

One unique common interest that Gann and Bayer shared as market speculators was an additional study of astrology in the markets, then and now referred to as astro cycles. Although we do not cover the subject of astro cycles in this book, it is worth noting an article by Lisa Burrell in the *Harvard Business Review* of November 2006 that cites research by Ilia D. Dichev and Troy D. Janes into stock prices during the 28.5-day cycle between a new moon and a full moon. The article says the cycle may have an application in predicting stock prices.

This is not at all surprising, given the fact that the markets are fueled by the energy of market participants. Changes in people's moods and behavior around moon cycles have been well documented throughout the years, and these can also be found in the changes of price behavior in the markets.

Even the legendary twentieth-century financier J. Pierpont Morgan was quoted as saying, "Millionaires don't use astrology, but billionaires do." For many years he employed a full-time financial astrologer by the name of Evangeline Adams.

Arch Crawford is probably the best-known of the contemporary market astrologists and has produced some of the most accurate market predictions, published in his newsletter *The Crawford Perspectives*. Crawford is a well-known and respected market technician in the trading arena today.

Another trader and important pioneer in using geometry in the markets was William Garrett. In 1972 his book *Torque Analysis of Stock Market Cycles* was published (it is now available through Traders Press). In this book Garrett describes the progression of a price chart. On page 89, he explains how it is dissected into triangles that lead through a normal progression of expansions. These expansions form a circle, which leads to the squaring of the circle (unifying the two shapes by making them equal in area or perimeter), leading to an ellipse. This is done through the progression of Fibonacci numbers:

- .618 – 1.618.
- 1.618 – 2.618.
- Pi, 3.14, which is the ratio of the circumference of a circle to its diameter.

We assure you the patterns we present in this book are not nearly as complicated as this may sound. Several extremely accomplished market technicians over the years have made a lifetime study of the markets through the use of geometry. Because of their breakthroughs and developments, we now have the patterns in this book rooted in geometry, sacred geometry, and the application of Fibonacci ratios. It should be noted here that the basis of sacred geometry is not one of a religious nature but rather one made up of the ratios, square roots, and reciprocals of the numbers 1 through 5.

FIBONACCI RATIOS

So what are Fibonacci ratios, and where did they come from? Let's start with what they are; we will go back to ancient times to answer this question. Pythagoras (ca. 580–500 B.C.E.) is considered to be the father of modern geometry. He was also a great philosopher of ancient Greece and founder of the Pythagorean brotherhood. He and his students believed and taught that reality is mathematical in nature. They believed that numbers and proportion were harmonic and that everything was related through mathematics. However, the mathematical system we use today was still many centuries away and was not used by Pythagoras and his students, so they were limited in proving their theories.

This belief in proportion and harmony has been intricately linked throughout history to what is referred to as the golden mean. Other terms for this include divine proportion, golden section, and golden ratio. These all refer to phi, which is the mathematical term to describe the proportion of the whole to its parts, which is considered to be the perfect proportion.

These teachings and many others of Pythagoras were passed down through the centuries. It is even alleged that the Freemasons were an offshoot of the secret school of Pythagoras.

If we move up the time line to circa 300 B.C.E., this was when one of the last great ancient Greek philosophers, Euclid, lived. He was the first to coherently express the golden mean as a mathematical ratio. Figure 2.4 is an illustration of this proportion. The line AB represents the whole. The ratio of AB to AC will be the same as the ratio of AC to CB. This calculates to a ratio of 1.618 to 1, which can also be referred to as phi, the golden mean.

The ratio and proportions of the golden mean are abundantly apparent in nature, music, art, science, and the cosmos. The Great Pyramid of Giza, one of the seven wonders of the world, is structured with these proportions. Other examples include the Parthenon and works of great artists such as Leonardo da Vinci, Rembrandt, and the nineteenth-century English artist J.M.W. Turner, to name a few. These are just a few. If you delve

FIGURE 2.4 Example of proportion using the golden mean ratio.

into art history books you will find a plethora of artists who employed these proportions seeking balance and harmony, some consciously and others intuitively.

In nature these proportions are endless. They live and grow around us in all corners of the world. Many species of flowers—sunflowers, roses, daisies—are all fantastically imbued with these proportions. Seashells, pineapples, and even our faces, bodies, and limbs are in proportion to the golden mean. If you were to measure the distance from your elbow to the tips of your fingers, then the distance between your fingertip to your wrist, and then wrist to elbow, these proportions would mirror the golden mean illustrated in Figure 2.4.

In the cosmos there are many examples of these proportions. Planets move in elliptical fashion, and their orbits coincide with the expansion of the Fibonacci summation series. An example is Earth's orbit in relation to the Venus/Uranus cycle. These planetary orbits possess the unique Fibonacci relationship of.618; it takes 225 days for Venus and Uranus to make a complete cycle from conjunction to conjunction. If we take 365 days (Earth's cycle) and multiply it by.618, we come out with 225. There are many relationships that repeat these same types of cycles, too numerous to list here.

On our time line we now move forward to Pisa, Italy, in the twelfth century A.D. It was here that Leonardo of Pisa (ca. 1170–1240) was born. He was brought up in times of a revived interest in education, especially in the Greek sciences and philosophies.

Leonardo was given the nickname "Fibonacci" posthumously, possibly derived from his father's name, Bonacci. At any rate, his name today is synonymous with the famous Fibonacci sequence.

Leonardo initially studied mathematics with a system derived from Roman numerals. He would soon make an enormous contribution to the evolution of mathematics that remains with us today. He had learned the Eastern (Indian) system of using nine numerals and studied intensively with mathematicians in several Mediterranean countries. It is known that Leonardo did travel to Egypt and studied the proportions of the pyramids, including Giza. It must have been of great interest to him to find that the dimensions of this great pyramid contain the Fibonacci ratios or golden mean.

Out of these studies he wrote a book called *Liber abaci* (*Book of Calculation*). This book introduced to the world, although one copy at a time, the system of using nine numerals. He expanded his impressive mathematical knowledge, and eventually this is what has been adopted and applied as the standard mathematical system we now use.

All calculations before this revolutionary system were done laboriously with an abacus. Errors, of course, were difficult to track, because one had to start over each time. His new mathematical symbols opened the doors for simplifying what had been complicated mathematical calculations—multiplication and division, not to mention mathematical problems beyond those. They also allowed for an enhanced commerce, with these new mathematical symbols enabling businesspeople to enrich their businesses. Commerce at the time was on the verge of flourishing in Europe.

The Fibonacci numbers came about from a problem with rabbits that Leonardo solved, which led to the discovery of the Fibonacci series. In his book *Liber abaci* a problem is solved regarding how many rabbits would be produced in one year's time beginning with two rabbits. The answer is what we know today as the Fibonacci summation series:

$$1, 1, 2, 3, 5, 8, 13, 21, 34, 55, 89, 144, 233, 377, 610, 987, 1,597, 2,584,$$
$$4,181, 6,765, 10,946\ldots$$

The sequence goes on into infinity. Each number is the sum of the two preceding numbers, such as: $1 + 1 = 2$; $1 + 2 = 3$; $2 + 3 = 5$; $3 + 5 = 8$. Many things are fascinating about this sequence, but in particular is the relationship it has to the golden mean. If you take two numbers past the eighth sequence and divide the smaller number into the larger, you will get .618.

Here are three examples:

1. $89 \div 144 = .618$
2. $987 \div 1,597 = .618$
3. $6,765 \div 10,946 = .618$

If you divide the larger number into the smaller number after the eighth sequence you will arrive at 1.618, which is one of the extension ratios you will see us using in the chart examples later in the book. For example:

$$377 \div 233 = 1.618$$

It took many years for Leonardo's contribution to take hold and change commerce, which was his vision, and propel the world of mathematics forward. It is doubtful that his vision could have included or that he could have known this incredible sequence would centuries later be applied to the art of speculation and trading markets.

In the next section of this chapter we take a look at the specific Fibonacci ratios we use on a daily basis in our chart patterns.

APPLYING THE FIBONACCI RATIOS

There are many Fibonacci ratios as you can imagine from looking at the Fibonacci sequence. We focus on just a few in our trading. In later chapters you will find many chart examples using these ratios.

These are the main Fibonacci ratios we use in the chart pattern structures:

- .618—Φ
- .786—square root of .618
- 1.000
- 1.272—square root of 1.618
- 1.618

We do look at and use occasionally some secondary ratios, and these are:

- .382—used mainly in trending conditions
- .500—used mainly in trending conditions
- .707—used with AB=CD patterns that complete between .618 and .786
- .886—square root of .786; used with AB=CD patterns completing below .786
- 2.000—used in markets expanding beyond 1.272 and 1.618 extension numbers

See Figure 2.5 for a chart example of how the Fibonacci ratios look as applied with a Fibonacci retracement tool. In this example we show the .382, .500, .618, .786, 1.000, 1.272, and 1.618. This is a standard setting using a Fibonacci retracement tool found in many software packages, and is generally the standard setting we use.

Now we can take a look at how these Fibonacci ratios look placed onto an actual price chart in Figure 2.6. You can see how the price reacted at each Fibonacci ratio level.

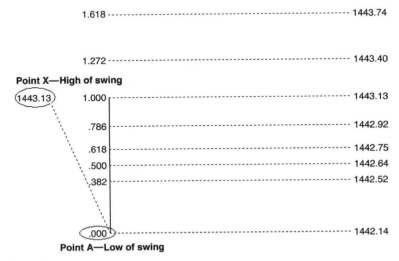

FIGURE 2.5 Example of Fibonacci ratios used.

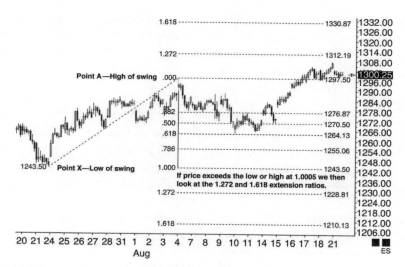

FIGURE 2.6 Example of Fibonacci ratios applied to a price chart.

This is a swing from low to high, and point X is the low of the swing. In this example the price found support almost exactly on the .618 level. This means that the price retraced down from the high of the swing at point A to the.618 price level. That is approximately two-thirds of the total swing length. A retracement of .382 is approximately one-third of the total swing length, and the .500 level is half of the swing length. The .786 level is approximately three-quarters of the entire swing length.

We want to note here that we do not always get a perfect support or resistance at a Fibonacci ratio, as you will see in the many chart examples in this book. We always use the ratios in combination with the various charting patterns and also with current market conditions—that is, a range trading environment (contracting) versus a trending environment (expanding).

The approach using geometric triangles is simple in that we are looking at points that connect from highs to lows and vice versa. Triangles that are contracting are contracting by the numbers of .618 and .786.

Triangles that are equal are those that have AB=CD legs (see Chapter 4 on the AB=CD pattern). The triangles that are expanding are expanding to the 1.272 and the 1.618 ratios. Patterns that have to be forced are usually in the asymmetrical category and should be avoided. There are many opportunities with well-formed symmetrical patterns, and the trader should focus on those. Refer back to Figure 2.3. As with any trading method, all trades are only a probability and never a certainty.

What you will observe as you study and learn these patterns is that some stocks and markets tend to repeat one Fibonacci ratio more than others. As an example, you may notice that a particular stock tends to trade to the .786 more frequently than the .618. Or you may notice one of the secondary numbers more frequently in one stock or market, such as the .707. It will be helpful to note these observations when you see them.

SUMMARY

As you can see in a review of this chapter, geometry and the price patterns formed are interchangeable. Geometry is an important foundation for each pattern presented in this book. The patterns are all triangles of varying degrees and sizes, and some we have given clever names to, such as the Gartley "222" pattern (Chapter 5) or the Butterfly pattern (Chapter 6).

The basic principles remain the same: These patterns are geometric; they repeat and can be quantified. As you study and gain experience, you will train your eye to the symmetrical versus the asymmetrical patterns.

As those of us who have studied and now apply these principles have learned, these patterns based in geometry have always been in the price chart, and it was a matter of someone teaching us how to see them. Our hope is that many of you reading this book who have never looked at a price chart from this perspective will be as taken as we were when we first learned about these phenomena.

CHAPTER 3

Harmonic Numbers and How to Use Them

Learning what harmonic numbers are and how to use them will be a key to your total understanding of market behavior and of the patterns we present in this book. Harmonic numbers are fascinating vibratory swings that occur in each market and each individual stock. Each market is made up of energy that is fueled by the market participants. This in turn creates swings of price that are measurable and repetitive.

This chapter covers what harmonic numbers are and how they are at the root of the basic pattern structures presented in this book. We take a look at the term *harmonic numbers* as it relates to price swings, and examine how you can apply harmonic numbers in your trading for entries, exits, and stop placements.

WHERE THE TERM *HARMONIC NUMBERS* ORIGINATED

Although harmonic numbers have been inherent in markets and individual stocks all along, the specific term came from Jim Twentyman. Twentyman, who was a broker at the Conti Commodity Trading office in Westwood, California, had studied W.D. Gann extensively and is considered an expert on Gann. He had worked for over a year in the

1970s at a bookstore called The Investment Center, which was located a short distance from the Conti Commodity Trading office. The bookstore had an extensive library of over 5,000 investment books. This gave Twentyman an opportunity to study all of Gann's works, including the astrology books Gann had worked on.

Twentyman's knowledge of numbers from sacred geometry evolved from these studies. He had worked with one of Gann's concepts of squaring price and time together. By utilizing Gann's square of 9 (which was a circle of 360 degrees divided into 12 30-degree segments) and the numbers from the Fibonacci summation series, he discovered what are now known as harmonic numbers. These are the numbers that repeat in all markets in all time frames.

DEFINING A HARMONIC NUMBER

Let's start with a definition of the word *harmonic* as it pertains to physics:

> *Har-mon-ic—Physics—Any component of a periodic oscillation whose frequency is an integral multiple of the fundamental frequency.*

As you study the markets or individual stocks, you will see that they do only one of three things at any given time:

1. Move up.
2. Move down.
3. Move sideways.

Markets are always in a process of either expanding or contracting. Generally, markets spend more time contracting—trading in a range, trading sideways, forming support and resistance areas—than they do in a trend. Refer to Figure 3.1 for an example of a sideways-trading market.

FIGURE 3.1   Example of a sideways market: Dow futures 60-minute chart.

FIGURE 3.2 Example of a downtrend: crude oil futures.

A trend can be defined as higher highs and higher lows for an uptrend, and lower highs and lower lows for a downtrend. See Figure 3.2 for an example of a downtrend and Figure 3.3 for an example of an uptrend. When markets are in a range they are *contracting*, and when they are in a trend they are *expanding*. Here is where we would like you to think in terms of vibrations, repetitions, and swings.

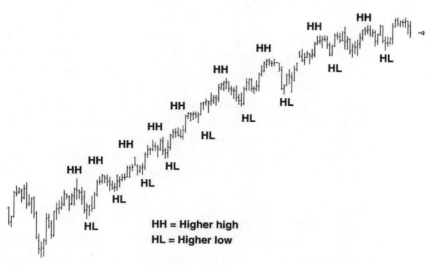

FIGURE 3.3 Example of an uptrend: Dow futures.

**This long (wide) range bar is
the reaction to an economic release.**

FIGURE 3.4 Dow futures 5-minute chart showing range expansion following an economic report.

VIBRATIONS IN PRICE SWINGS

Vibrations in the markets can be thought of as sound waves. The louder the sound, the farther it will travel. Eventually the sound will lose momentum as it travels, and the momentum will dissipate. The same analogy could be used describing an object being dropped. The larger the object and the greater the distance it is dropped, the larger the vibration that is created as it meets with a surface. Price movement is very similar to this. As an example, a release of an economic report or news-related item could cause prices to suddenly thrust up or down. Figure 3.4 shows an example of a price thrust or expansion after the release of an economic report. Shocks such as natural disasters, currency devaluations, and wars are extreme events that will have larger vibration effects on the markets.

When prices have stayed within a range for a while, it is a matter of time before they move away from that range. Many times prices will move away from the range with urgency in the form of a trend. (See Chapter 10 on trends.) Figure 3.5 is an example of a range that formed, and when price broke to the downside out of the range, it did so in a decisive manner that was evident in the long (wide) range bars.

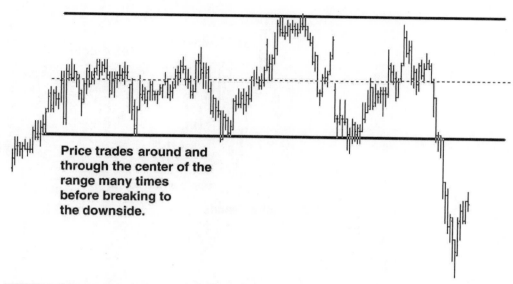

Price trades around and through the center of the range many times before breaking to the downside.

FIGURE 3.5 S&P E-mini 15-minute chart. Price moves away from the trading range in the form of a trend.

Using the price behavior from Figure 3.5 as an example, the price contracted as it formed the range and expanded as it broke the low price support area; it then began trending. What we can say is that strong vibrations can equal a trend, while milder to weaker vibrations will form a range. The trading range can also be thought of as stored energy. Eventually this energy will have to be released in one direction or another. The milder and weaker vibrations usually will not have enough strength to sustain a trend.

It is possible to see increased volatility that creates strong vibrations or price swings. The market will trade in both directions as market participants battle back and forth until a winner is decided. Once the winner has taken control (either bulls or bears), the price can have very strong vibratory movements (such as a trend move) in one direction as the losing side liquidates positions and new participants in the direction of the trend pile in.

Figure 3.6 shows dramatic swings in the gold futures weekly chart as bulls and bears battle over the direction. Considering that each 1-point move in gold equals $100 per contract, these moves are significant.

Market participants will attach varying degrees of emotional meaning to the price as it moves up and down. As an example, if one side, such as bulls, participates in large numbers on the long side of the market (aggressive buying), that would create a stronger uptrend move or vibration in price (Figure 3.3). The opposite would be true for a strong downtrend move (Figure 3.2).

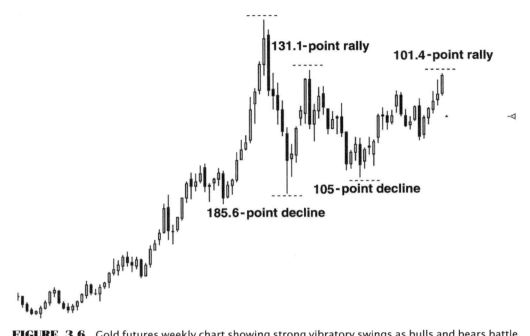

FIGURE 3.6   Gold futures weekly chart showing strong vibratory swings as bulls and bears battle.

REPETITION IN PRICE SWINGS

Using the patterns presented in this book, we find that the swings or vibratory moves in price are what we refer to as harmonic. They are price swings that are similar in length, are repetitive, and are found in all time frames. Figure 3.7 shows a 60-minute chart of the Dow futures. At first glance, this price movement can appear chaotic in nature: random upswings and downswings. In fact, many traders would not consider trading a chart with this appearance.

If we look at the same price chart and pick out the repetitive swings, we immediately impose order onto chaos. Referring to Figure 3.8, what we have done is use a line drawing tool in the software program; we have cloned the line and dropped it onto the swings. We have not changed or altered the length of the original line; we have simply moved it onto each repetitive swing. What you see in Figure 3.8 are harmonic swings of the 60-minute price chart of the Dow futures. This clearly illustrates the repetition that is present in this market on this time frame.

Let's look at a few more charts illustrating these repetitions. Figure 3.9 is a 15-minute chart of IBM. This chart shows repetitive upswings. The two swings form an AB=CD pattern, which is the first pattern we will present (see Chapter 4, "The AB=CD Pattern.")

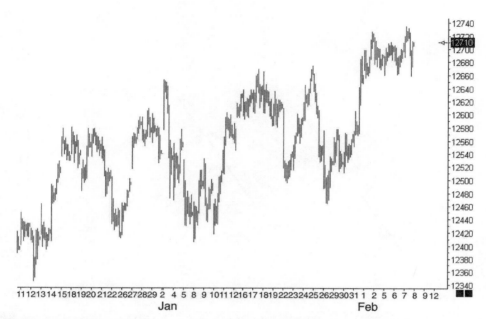

FIGURE 3.7 Dow futures 60-minute chart showing seemingly random swings.

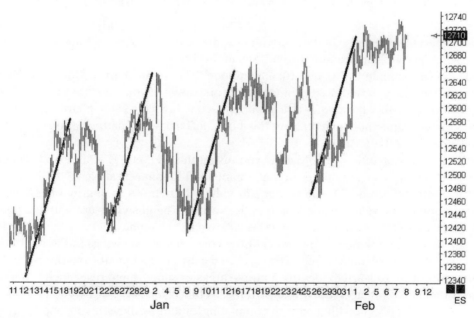

FIGURE 3.8 Dow futures 60-minute chart. Example of applying cloned lines to find the harmonic swings.

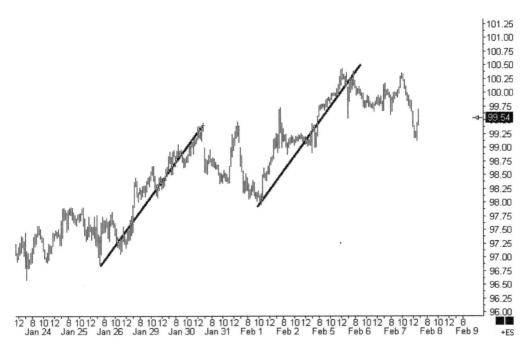

FIGURE 3.9 IBM 15-minute chart showing harmonic swings forming an AB=CD pattern.

You can start to get a sense of the importance of these harmonic swings and the role they will play in learning and trading the patterns in this book.

The next example is Figure 3.10, a 30-minute time frame chart of Google. It shows repetitive swings or harmonics forming both up and down. If you study the chart, you will notice a set of smaller harmonics that form the second upswing in the chart. Again, those swings are forming another pattern in this book, a Gartley sell pattern. (See Chapter 5, "The Gartley '222' Pattern.")

Later in this chapter we will show you, using the S&P 500 E-mini, variations of a harmonic number using multiples of that number and Fibonacci ratios.

The S&P 500 E-mini 60-minute chart in Figure 3.11 shows the harmonic swings in terms of points, as well as equal length in the swings. The upswings are within 2 points of each other and the corrective swings down are within 1 point.

Also interesting to note is that each of the corrective downswings in Figure 3.11 relate to the .618 retracement levels. They are each a .618 retracement from the swing low to high. You want to learn to identify multiple areas of support and resistance using harmonic numbers, Fibonacci ratios, and patterns. At times you may have several Fibonacci ratios at one price level with a pattern completing, and most likely if you also study the harmonics you will find those present as well.

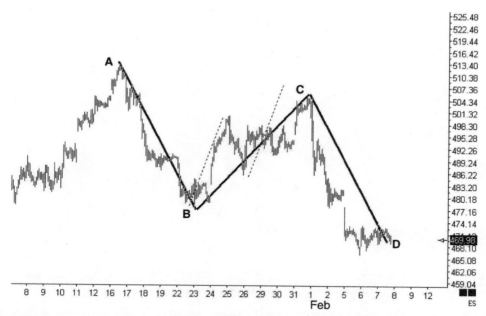

FIGURE 3.10 Google 30-minute chart showing harmonic swings forming in both directions.

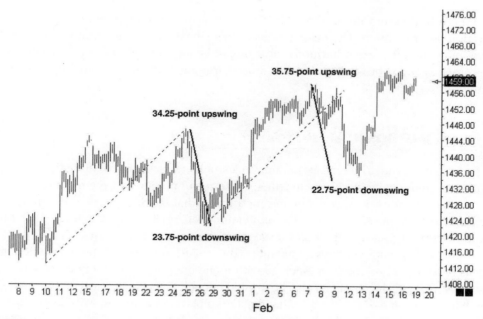

FIGURE 3.11 S&P 500 E-mini 60-minute chart showing the harmonic swings in terms of point moves.

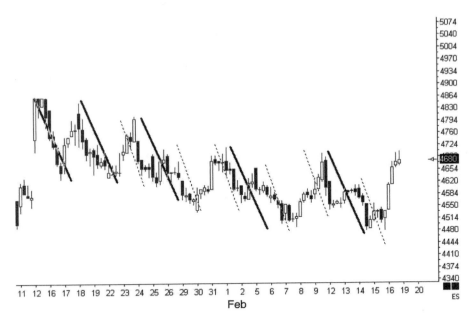

FIGURE 3.12 Wheat futures 60-minute chart showing repetition, vibration, and smaller harmonic within a larger harmonic.

Figure 3.12 shows an easy-to-identify example of harmonic numbers that include vibration and repetition. The dashed lines in this wheat futures chart show the smaller harmonic within the larger harmonic or swing. It is not unusual to see this occurrence, where one swing is broken into two or more harmonic swings that make up the larger harmonic.

FINDING HARMONIC NUMBERS

To find the harmonic or vibratory number in a stock or market is not difficult. You want to find the common swings using length, or in terms of points, that recur over and over. You are looking for the most common repetition in that stock or market. If you trade a particular time frame such as a 5-, 15-, or 30-minute chart (it does not matter which time frame you trade), you want to look for the repetition on that time frame.

Using a 30-minute chart as an example, the easiest way to find the harmonic numbers is to look for and mark in (such as with a line drawing tool) the most common or repetitive swings. The chart can also be printed out and the swings drawn in by hand. We feel that doing some of this work by hand makes a better connection with the brain, and helps train the eye for identifying these swings.

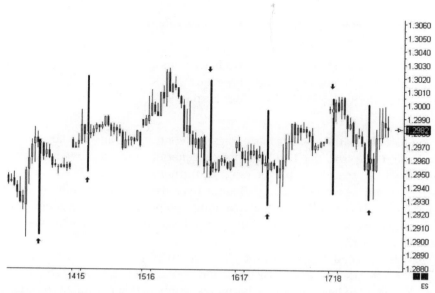

FIGURE 3.13   Vertical lines represent a 70-pip swing in euro currency futures 30-minute chart.

In the 30-minute chart of the euro currency, there is a common swing (harmonic number) of approximately 70 pips (pip, or price interest point, refers to the smallest unit of price movement. In the euro currency one pip is equal to $12.50). In Figure 3.13, the vertical lines each represent 70 pips (the arrows on the chart indicate whether the line is showing an upswing or a downswing). You can see that some of these swings are almost exact and others are just a bit off the mark, but still close to the 70-pip harmonic in that market. Keep in mind that the price swings will not always be to the exact number. Think of these numbers as areas or zones that you watch for the price to move toward.

If you study at least 100 samples of this particular swing in the euro currency, you will discover that the swings will be related to this 70-pip harmonic number by the expansion or contraction numbers of .618, .786, 1.272, or 1.618. Finding one-half of this harmonic, 35 pips, in the euro is not at all uncommon, just as one-half of the harmonic is easily found in the wheat chart (Figure 3.12).

Harmonic Numbers in the S&P 500

These are the harmonic numbers that we use for the S&P 500 market:

- 5.4 points—a primary harmonic number in this market.
- 6.85 points—derived using 5.4×1.272.
- 8.7 points—derived using 1.618×5.4.

Beyond this, then look at multiples such as 10.8 and larger harmonic numbers:

- 10.8 points—derived using 5.4 × 2 (two harmonics).
- 16.2 points—derived using 5.4 × 3 (three harmonics).
- 21.6 points—derived using 5.4 × 4 (four harmonics).

As you can guess, the smaller harmonics are contraction and the larger harmonics are expansion. Price over the 10.8 harmonic is generally a trend mode and can expand on an intraday basis to the 16.2 to 21.6 range or further.

When the market is in a trend (see Chapter 10 on trend identification for the S&P 500 market), the corrections will be in the 1.75-point to 5-point range as a general rule. One of the common contractions we see on these trend days is 3.5 points, which is .618 of the 5.4 harmonic number.

On very strong trend days we see the 1.75-point to 2.5-point corrections, which are related to the square roots of 5.4 and 3.5; the square root of 5.4 is 2.32, and the square root of 3.5 is 1.87. You want to be aware of the harmonic numbers that pertain to the type of trading day you have—range-trading day (contraction) versus a trend-mode day (expansion).

Figure 3.14 shows an excellent example of the common swings using harmonic numbers we see using a 5-minute chart of the S&P 500. You can easily see how each swing was within the harmonic ranges and the repetition that occurred.

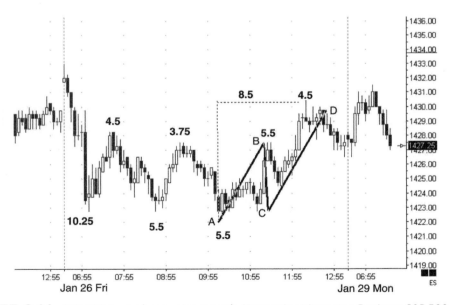

FIGURE 3.14 S&P 500 E-mini harmonics at work. Harmonic swings on a 5-minute S&P 500 chart.

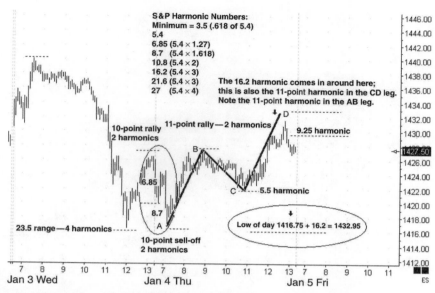

S&P Harmonic Numbers:
Minimum = 3.5 (.618 of 5.4)
5.4
6.85 (5.4 × 1.27)
8.7 (5.4 × 1.618)
10.8 (5.4 × 2)
16.2 (5.4 × 3)
21.6 (5.4 × 3)
27 (5.4 × 4)

The 16.2 harmonic comes in around here; this is also the 11-point harmonic in the CD leg. Note the 11-point harmonic in the AB leg.

10-point rally 2 harmonics

11-point rally—2 harmonics

9.25 harmonic

6.85

8.7

C----5.5 harmonic

23.5 range—4 harmonics

10-point sell-off 2 harmonics

Low of day 1416.75 + 16.2 = 1432.95

FIGURE 3.15 Large ranges of harmonic numbers over a two-day period.

If you look at the dashed line area in Figure 3.14, you will see how the first leg up of that swing was a 5.5-point swing; this was followed by a 4.5-point swing. The total leg was 8.5 points, with the low at 1422 and the high of the swing at 1430.50.

Another example of the harmonics in the S&P 500 is shown in Figure 3.15. In this example we see a large range of the harmonic numbers over a short time period of two days. We see a corrective move up that formed an AB=CD sell pattern. (See Chapter 4, "The AB=CD Pattern.") When we see this type of pattern form using the harmonic numbers, we also want to combine Fibonacci ratios to help us find additional areas of support or resistance, in this case resistance.

The corrective pattern completed very close to the 16.2 harmonic numbers (within 1.25 points), at the .618 level, as seen in Figure 3.16. By combining these two resistance levels—the harmonic numbers and the .618 Fibonacci retracement level—we are able to then determine the entry point and stop placement for this type of setup.

It is worth repeating that we are not trying to find exact harmonic numbers to the tick to enter trades. We are working with ranges, price zones, and common areas of support or resistance. We use the harmonic numbers as a tool in conjunction with the patterns and the Fibonacci ratios.

When to Use Expansions of Harmonic Numbers

Since harmonic numbers are repetitive and are part of vibrations in the markets, and we know that the price will not remain in a range forever, then we must look at occurrences

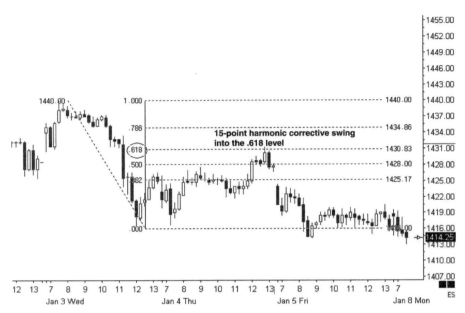

FIGURE 3.16 Combining Fibonacci ratios with harmonic numbers in S&P 500 E-mini 15-minute chart.

when we see expansion and then look at multiples of the harmonic numbers. Practical experience has shown that once a market goes beyond its primary harmonic number, then that market or stock can see a multiple of two to three times that harmonic number and sometimes more. This is related to a concept Gann worked on, which was the concept of overbalancing. When both price and time exceeded normal corrections, the main trend has most probably changed. This may be seen on a lower time frame first and then on the longer-term time frames as price continues to reverse.

Using the 3 Percent Rule for Finding a Harmonic Number and Practical Applications

Another method for finding the harmonic numbers in a stock or market is to use 3 percent of the value of the stock, commodity, or currency. If we use IBM as an example (see Figure 3.17), the first swing shows a high at $99.48. The 3 percent harmonic would be approximately $2.98 (this can be rounded up or down a few cents). The market retraced approximately one-half of that harmonic, or $1.52. We can use $2.98 for placing a stop-loss order if buying the pullback. Conversely, if short from that high, then the $2.98 could also be used for placing a stop-loss order.

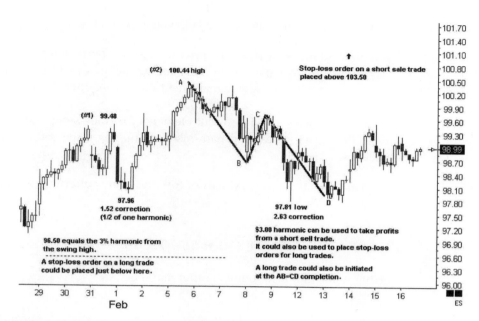

FIGURE 3.17 Using harmonic numbers for placing stop-loss orders and initiating trades in an IBM 60-minute chart.

The area in Figure 3.17 marked #2 has a harmonic number using 3 percent of $100.44 per share, or approximately $3.00. We would then look for a pullback of approximately $3.00 per share. This area can be used as a profit target area for any short sales from the swing highs.

Figure 3.17 also shows an AB=CD pattern (see Chapter 4, "The AB=CD Pattern") that formed into the area of the harmonic number. Again, this combines two elements: harmonic numbers and a pattern. The trader, if initiating a long trade, could then use the harmonic of $3.00 to place a stop-loss order.

Let's review the different applications of the harmonic numbers in Figure 3.17:

- If the trader had entered a short trade near the swing highs, a stop-loss order could be placed just beyond the harmonic $3.00 per share (3 percent).
- A projection down from the highs, using the harmonic number, could be used to take profits from a short-sale trade.
- A long trade could be initiated at the completion of the AB=CD pattern, which is also at the $3.00 harmonic.
- A stop-loss order can be placed on long trades in this example using the $3.00 harmonic.

Using harmonic numbers as a guideline should help you in several ways:

- They can help you understand the rhythm and price swings of a particular market.
- They should help you in stop-loss placement by reducing risk in a trade to a manageable level and within specific money management guidelines. (See Chapter 11, "Trade Management.")
- You're aware of the combinations and different elements for trade setups, such as harmonic numbers, Fibonacci ratios, and patterns for initiating trade setups, and taking profit objectives.

Finally, harmonic numbers are an integral part of forming many patterns presented in this book.

HARMONIC NUMBERS FOUND IN OTHER MARKETS

Here are some of the harmonic numbers found in other markets:

- Bond market—20 ticks.
- Crude oil—44 and 88.
- Dow Jones—35, 105, and 70.
- Euro market—35 and 70.
- Gold market—11 and 17.
- Silver market—18, 36, and 12.
- Wheat—11 and 17.
- Soybeans—18 and 36.

Use multiples of these numbers in strong markets. Remember that different variations of these numbers will be found in swings depending on whether the market is contracting or expanding. The harmonic for a 5-minute chart may vary as opposed to a 30-minute chart. They will be related, however, by percentages. The harmonic on a smaller time frame such as a 5-minute chart may be one-half or .618 percent of the larger harmonic number.

The only way to learn is to observe these numbers for yourself. If on a daily basis you were to track the swings in any given market on a 5-, 15-, or 30-minute chart and keep a record, you would then begin to see the repetitions that occur frequently. If you did this over a 30-day period, you would see almost every type of pattern occur within that time period: up, down, and sideways, contracting and expanding. You would also see the theory of harmonic numbers unfold and the relationship they have to the Fibonacci summation series.

The basic geometry, Fibonacci ratios, and harmonic numbers, as you will see, are the foundations for the patterns presented in Chapters 4 through 10.

PART II

The Price Patterns and How to Trade Them

CHAPTER 4

The AB=CD
Pattern

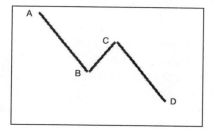

It has been said many times in trading to study, learn, and trade methods that are simple in nature. The AB=CD pattern is one of the most basic and simple patterns in technical analysis. If the trader will take the time to learn this pattern and its variations, it will be time well spent.

We teach you this pattern here both in structure and from a trading standpoint using real chart examples. In coming chapters we show you how this simple pattern is also formed within other patterns such as the Gartley "222" pattern, Butterfly pattern, Three Drives pattern, and some of the classic technical analysis patterns.

HISTORY OF THE AB=CD PATTERN

In 1935 a book was published for sale to investors at an incredible price of $1,500. That book was *Profits in the Stock Market* by H.M. Gartley. On page 249, under "Practical Use of Trend Lines," Gartley describes a chart pattern that we now call the AB=CD pattern. (See Figure 4.1.)

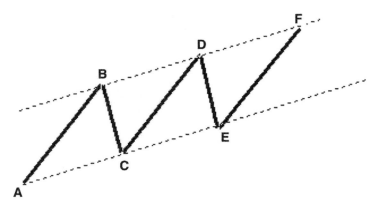

FIGURE 4.1 Illustration of the Parallel Trend Lines chart found in H.M. Gartley's book, *Profits in the Stock Market* (1935).
Courtesy of Lambert Gann Publishing. P.O. Box 0, Pomeroy, WA 99347. www.wdgann.com.

This pattern has appeared in another work, one by Frank Tubbs. Tubbs offered a correspondence course in the 1950s called *The Frank Tubbs Stock Market Course*. This course was based on the pattern that Gartley had explained in his 1935 book.

Tubbs used many charts from the 1920s and 1930s in his description of the pattern and brought the work forward into the 1950s, validating this classic pattern. Charles Lindsay also used this pattern in his book *Trident: A Trading Strategy* written in 1976. Lindsay identified trends as micro, minor, intermediate, and major. He illustrated that the parallel price swings were apparent on all charts and in all time frames. The system described was identical to Gartley's pattern. Lindsay labeled his pattern with P1, P2, P3, and P4, which were nothing more than A, B, C, and D.

Lindsay took the AB=CD pattern and made it into a formula that would give the pattern a completion target at D (P4), so the formula would be:

$$P4 = \frac{P2 + P3}{P1}$$

This is equivalent to:

$$D = \frac{B + C}{A}$$

He then came up with a formula that said P3 should be a ratio of .625 of P1 to P2. This is equivalent to a .618 retracement by the BC leg from the AB swing. (See Figure 4.2.) He took 25 percent of the P1 or the first leg as a risk factor.

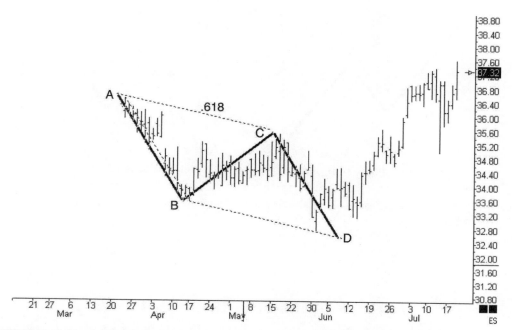

FIGURE 4.2 Merck (MRK) daily chart showing AB=CD pattern with .618 retracement of the AB leg. This is similar to Lindsay's .625 retracement of the P1 to P2 leg.

AB=CD PATTERN DESCRIPTION

Gartley's description of the AB=CD pattern illustrated how the market would rally in an uptrend and then retrace. It would then rally to another uptrend then make another retracement, forming an upsloping parallel channel. It was from this description that the AB=CD pattern achieved its nickname, the lightning bolt. (See Figure 4.1.)

Gartley spent several pages referring to these trend lines and parallel lines as excellent signals when used in conjunction with other working tools. He also applied these lines to price ratios. He used mainly ratios of one-third and one-half for retracements.

AB=CD PATTERN STRUCTURE

The AB=CD pattern is found in all markets and all time frames. This pattern is the foundation for the Gartley buy and sell patterns (discussed in Chapter 5). It is also an integral part of the Butterfly pattern (Chapter 6) and also forms a part of the Three Drives pattern (Chapter 7). The pattern is a measured move where the CD leg is similar in length to the

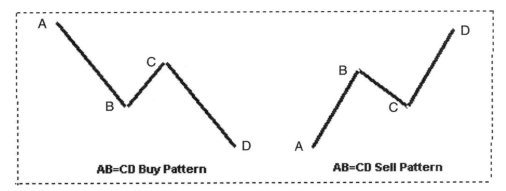

FIGURE 4.3a Basic structure of the AB=CD pattern, illustrating the "lightning bolt" shape of the buy and sell patterns.

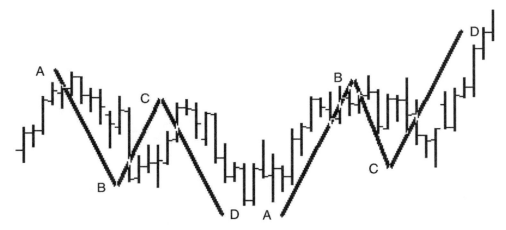

FIGURE 4.3b AB=CD buy and sell patterns with S&P E-mini chart price.

AB leg. It should be noted, though, that the CD leg can extend and will not always be exactly equal to the AB leg; this is discussed in "Important Characteristics of the AB=CD Pattern" later in this chapter. Figure 4.3 shows the shape of the basic AB=CD buy and sell patterns.

There are three legs that form this pattern. (See Figure 4.4.) The first leg of the pattern is labeled AB. After the completion of the first leg, a retracement or correction occurs that will usually find support or resistance at one of these Fibonacci levels: .382, .50, .618, or .786. This correction or retracement is labeled BC and is the second leg of the pattern. (Note: Strongly trending markets will usually see only a retracement to the .382 level. See the chart in the "Slope and Time Frames" section later in the chapter for an example of a shallow retracement at the .382 level.)

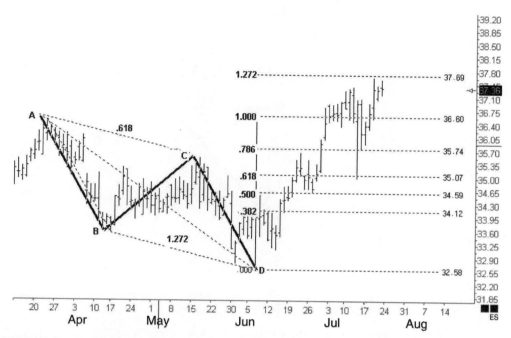

FIGURE 4.4 Merck (MRK) daily chart showing completed AB=CD pattern. This pattern completion leads to retracements of the AD swing of almost all the main Fibonacci levels we use.

When price resumes in the same direction as the AB leg, the CD leg then begins to form. Once we identify the CD leg forming, we can project the potential pattern completion and devise a trading strategy. As the CD leg forms and completes, we monitor the final leg for any warning signs that would alert us to a change in market conditions that may signal us to possibly pass on the trade or wait for further confirmation before entering the trade. Chapter 11, "Trade Management," covers this in more detail. Once the price exceeds B, we make an assumption that the price will reach pattern completion at point D.

When studying this pattern, it is important to know what invalidates the pattern. Here are three items that would invalidate the AB=CD pattern:

1. BC cannot exceed the AB leg, meaning the retracement of AB cannot exceed 1.00.
2. BC can be a 1.00 retracement of the AB leg; this is a rare pattern and a double top or bottom, but it is a valid pattern.
3. D must exceed B in order for the pattern to complete at point D and be a valid AB=CD pattern. See Figure 4.5 as an example.

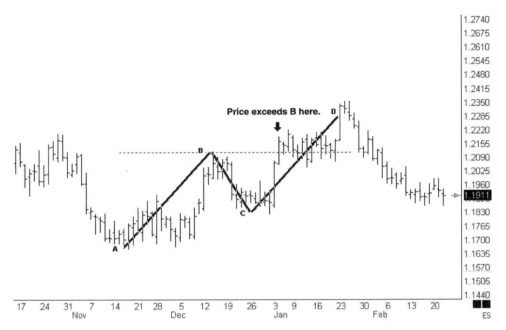

FIGURE 4.5 Euro daily chart. Once price exceeds B, we assume the pattern will complete at point D.

IMPORTANT CHARACTERISTICS OF THE AB=CD PATTERN

About 40 percent of the time, the AB=CD pattern will be perfectly symmetrical, meaning AB equals CD. The other 60 percent of the time variations of the pattern will be present. What this means is that after the AB leg has formed and the retracement leg, BC, has completed, the CD leg will be different from the AB leg. The two legs may or may not be perfectly symmetrical.

Some of the ways the CD leg can vary from the AB leg include:

- The CD leg is an extension of AB anywhere from 1.27 to 2.00 (or greater). See Figure 4.6 as an example.
- The CD leg has a slope or angle steeper or wider than AB.

At first glance this variation might make the trader think the pattern is not tradable. The key lies in identifying the BC leg. The most important thing is to watch the price action coming after point C has formed. Many of the examples that you will see in this chapter will show that the CD leg determines the relationship to the AB leg.

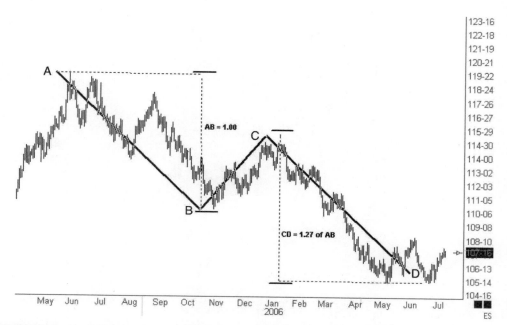

FIGURE 4.6 Daily chart of 30-year bonds showing AB=CD pattern with the CD leg extending to 1.27 of the AB leg.

CD LEG VARIATIONS

These CD leg phenomena can be described in four ways:

1. If after point C has occurred a gap exists in the direction of point D, this usually indicates that the CD leg will be much greater than the AB leg—1.272, 1.618, or more. See Figure 4.7 as an example.

2. A wide range bar (twice normal size) at point C is another indication that the CD leg could become extended. See Figure 4.8 as an example.

3. Ideally, AB=CD moves are symmetrical in price and time. For example, if the AB leg is six bars up, then the CD leg will be six bars up. See Figure 4.9 as an example.

4. As illustrated in Figure 4.10, the time to form the two legs is symmetrical.

This next sentence is very important: If the CD leg is made in just a few bars, this strongly indicates that the CD leg is going to be an expansion of the AB leg. See Figure 4.11 for an example of this.

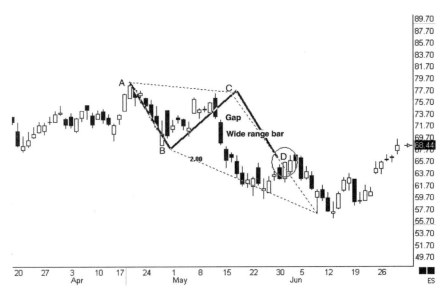

FIGURE 4.7 Classic AB=CD pattern on EOG Resources (EOG) daily chart with gap from point C and sharp sloping down move to point D suggests CD leg will extend.

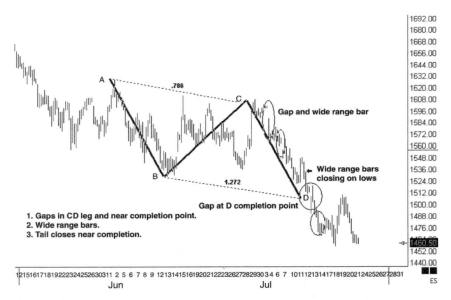

FIGURE 4.8 All the warning signs are present in this 120-minute chart of the NASDAQ futures. (Warning signs are discussed in Chapter 11.) Notice the long bars as the CD leg is just beginning down. This gives the trader an alert that the CD leg may be an extension to 1.272, 1.618, or greater of the AB leg.

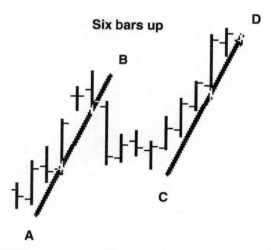

FIGURE 4.9 Euro currency daily chart showing AB=CD pattern with very symmetrical six bars up in the AB leg and six bars up in the CD leg.

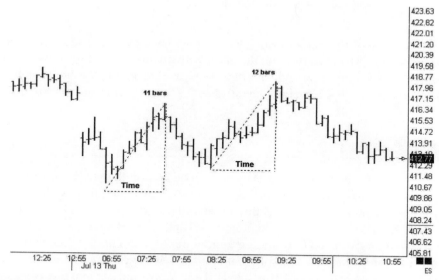

FIGURE 4.10 Google (GOOG) 5-minute chart showing time is also an element in the symmetry of the patterns.

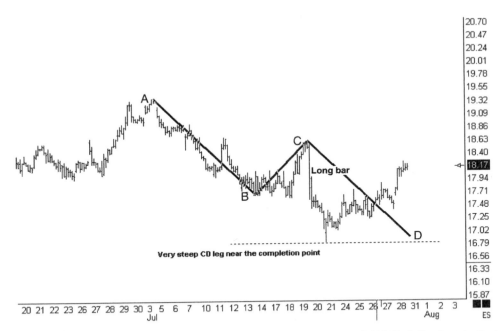

FIGURE 4.11 A very long bar from the C turning point in this Intel (INTC) daily chart indicates that the CD leg will be an expansion of the AB leg.

As an example of this thrust principle, imagine having two Ferrari automobiles on the racetrack, one with diesel fuel and the other with high-tech gasoline. It would be easy to understand the Ferrari powered with high-tech gasoline getting to the finish line first. Watch the CD leg, because if it starts fast, that is the faster Ferrari going further faster.

SLOPE AND TIME FRAMES

The slope or time frame of the BC move can also be helpful in determining the pattern. BC legs generally correct to one of the Fibonacci ratios: .382, .50, .618, or .786. The slope of this BC leg is usually a good indication of what the next CD leg will be. For example, assume that the AB leg took 15 trading bars to reach point B, and now the BC leg has taken 8 bars but has retraced only .382 percent of the AB leg. This is a sign of the market absorbing a lot of selling at a high price; it is a shallow retracement, and the price has not been able to retrace to .50, .618, or .786 percent. We would assume that prices would go much higher and possibly quite rapidly once the selling slows. However, if the market retraces to a .618 or .786 retracement, the CD leg will most probably be a normal move equaling AB=CD.

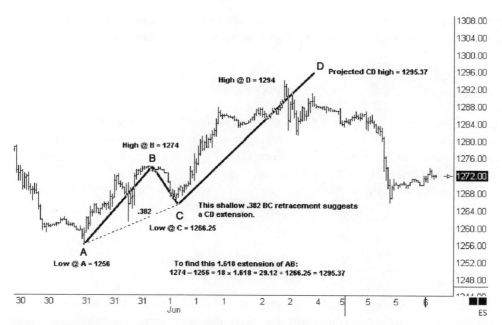

FIGURE 4.12 In this S&P E-mini 30-minute chart, the 1.618 extension can be figured by taking the difference between the high and low of AB, multiplying it by 1.618, and adding it to the low (or subtracting it from the high) of C.

To figure the extension of the CD leg, take the difference between A and B and multiply it by 1.272 or 1.618; then add the resulting figure to the low (or subtract it from the high) of C. The steps in Figure 4.12 to find the 1.618 projection would be calculated like this:

- B = 1274 − A = 1256 = 18 points
- 18 points × 1.618 = 29.12
- Add this to the low of C: 1266.25 + 29.12 = 1295.37

(If figuring 1.272 or any other extension number, simply use that number in place of 1.618.)

The number of time bars in the AB=CD pattern will usually range from five to eight bars. When the CD leg is extending beyond eight bars in an up or down move, the probability is for a price extension where CD will be 1.272, 1.618, or greater of the AB swing.

The examples in this chapter give a good point of reference to study these types of patterns. The reader should keep in mind that these patterns are only probabilities; they are not certainties, and trying to use these patterns without a solid understanding of them and a sound money management strategy is equivalent to trading suicide.

PSYCHOLOGY OF THE AB=CD PATTERN

Classic crowd psychology also forms the legs of the AB=CD pattern. There are two mechanisms that make the market move up and down—more buyers or more sellers; this is the ultimate greed barometer. Since fear is a stronger emotion than greed, markets tend to go down faster than they go up.

Price action in any actively traded market can be broken down into three steps:

1. Up moves.
2. Down moves.
3. Sideways moves.

The AB=CD pattern contains all three of these movements in a simple geometric form. Its trading value comes from its repetitive nature. It measures buying enthusiasm and selling climaxes.

Using an AB=CD sell pattern as an example (refer back to Figure 4.5), as the price begins to rise in the AB leg it catches the interest of those wanting to be in early. This could be early buying from large money sources such as mutual funds, pensions, and so on. As the price continues to rise, speculators may take note and climb on board, causing the price to rise further into the AB leg. Toward the top of the AB leg, individual investors (the general public) may start buying, not wanting to miss the move. There may be some news items on the individual stock or market, further drawing attention to the price rise. It is usually the case that this is toward the end of the first leg. Once the first leg is complete, some profit taking occurs and the price begins down. Those who bought near the top of this leg are now at a loss and some fear begins to set in, which can increase the selling.

As the price declines toward the Fibonacci retracement levels, those who may have missed the first move up begin to step in to buy the dip. Institutional investors may add to their positions, and speculators also may step in to buy a higher low, providing price support. The selling subsides, and the price finds support as more new buyers come into the stock or market and the price begins to resume its rise (CD leg). At this point some investors who rode out the loss from buying near the top of the AB leg may sell as the price approaches their breakeven point on the retracements back up from the BC leg. Some who missed getting out at a profit near the top of the AB leg now take profits as the price is close to those levels again.

The CD leg now begins to repeat the cycle of buyers, and as the price rises further those who realized they sold too soon may jump back in. A new surge of buying (or selling) will then push the price through the B point to complete the pattern at D.

TRADING THE AB=CD PATTERN

The AB=CD pattern can be found and traded in any time frame. We will show you examples of how we approach trading this pattern, including examples of both winning and losing trades. Here we show trade chart examples and trade management that could be applied to each trade; ultimately it is up to the individual trader to use a well thought-out and studied trading plan. (See Chapter 13, "Building a Trading Plan.")

We use two contracts in the futures or commodities markets trades to illustrate examples of scaling out in two parts, and also present an alternate trade management example using one exit. The stock examples use 200 shares to illustrate scaling out in two parts.

Trade Setup #1: AB=CD Sell Pattern

Market: S&P 500 E-mini

Contracts: 2

In the trade shown in Figure 4.13, the S&P E-mini market completes a picture-perfect AB=CD sell pattern. A limit order would be used on this entry at approximately 1286 to go short, just below the completion point at D. Once the order is filled, a stop-loss buy order is placed 5 points above the entry. In this case the stop-loss buy order would be placed at 1291.

The first exit is at the .618 retracement of the AD swing. We shade the exit order, meaning we place orders just above or below the actual exit, just as we do the entry orders, about .50 to 1 point away to try to ensure a fill. The exit order would be placed at 1279.50, just above the .618 retracement. Occasionally the market may trade just at but not through the price, and it will be up to the individual trader's discretion how to handle these situations. We prefer to exit if the price is traded at, even if it means slightly less profit. We don't want a winning trade to turn into a losing trade.

Risk-Free Trade   Once a profit is realized on the first part, the stop-loss order is then moved to the breakeven point. This accomplishes two very important things:

1. Reduces the risk in the trade.
2. Books a profit.

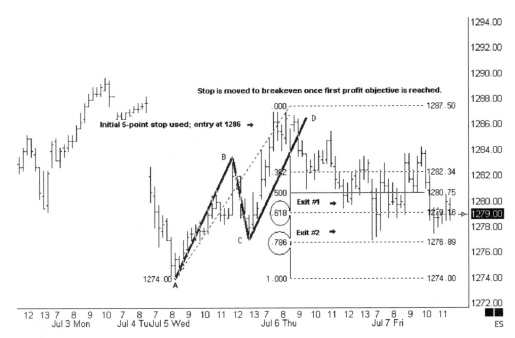

FIGURE 4.13 This is a picture-perfect S&P E-mini day trade of the AB=CD sell pattern. The market turns down almost exactly at the completion of D (15-minute chart).

At this point in the trade we have a 6.5-point profit and our stop has been moved to the breakeven point. Our second profit objective is at the .786 retracement level from the A–D swing. We place a limit order to exit the second contract at 1277.25, just above the .786 retracement level. Once the second profit objective is filled, we then remove our stop-loss order. The second contract profit nets 8.75 points for a total profit of 15.25 points.

Alternate Trade Management   As mentioned earlier, there are many ways to manage trades. In this particular example, a trader could choose to exit both contracts at the initial .618 profit objective. In this case the trader would have netted +13 points. In terms of 5 points being risked initially for a total of 10 points of risk, this is perfectly acceptable trade management. If the trade had been stopped out after the first profit objective was reached, then the trader would have netted +6.5 points on the trade. We have found that it is best to take profits when available and not worry about what the market does after you have reached your profit objectives. Always keep in mind that you are trading to make profits. In our trading we use both methods to exit our trades. Which method we use depends on current market conditions.

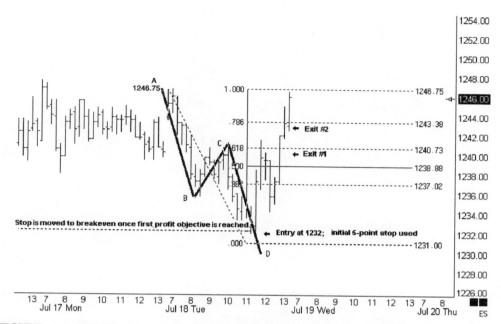

FIGURE 4.14 S&P E-mini 15-minute chart showing an AB=CD buy pattern trade where shading the order just above the actual completion point definitely helped us to get into the trade.

Trade Setup #2: AB=CD Buy Pattern

Market: S&P 500 E-mini

Contracts: 2

The S&P E-mini buy pattern setup shown in Figure 4.14 is a very good example of why we want to shade the orders to try to ensure a fill. This trade has an entry at 1232. Once the order is filled, an initial 5-point sell stop is placed. The first objective is easily reached within two time bars. On the chart you can see the long bar up from the entry point; this gives an indication that the price will make it to the .618 retracement. Once the first profit objective is reached, the stop is moved to breakeven to protect profits and to put us in a risk-free trade. The second profit objective is at the .786 retracement. Once the second profit objective is reached, the stop-loss order is canceled and that trade is over. This particular trade would have netted the trader +19 points.

Alternate Trade Management A full exit at the .618 level would have been a perfectly acceptable way to manage this trade. That would have given the trader a net profit of 16 points.

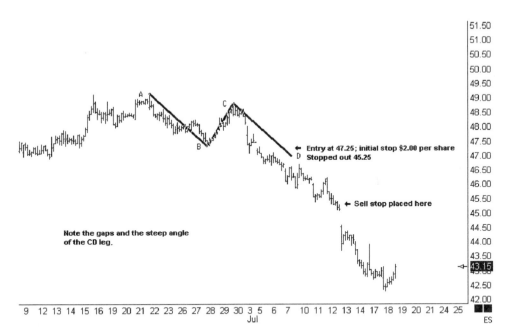

FIGURE 4.15   This AB=CD buy pattern trade (60-minute chart) of Wal-Mart (WMT) stock illustrates a very important point: Always use stop-loss orders.

Trade Setup #3: 60-Minute Failed AB=CD Buy Pattern

Market: Wal-Mart (WMT) Stock

Shares: 200

An example of a failed AB=CD buy pattern is shown in Figure 4.15. As noted on the chart, there are gaps and a steep CD leg down to the completion point. Sooner or later traders will find themselves in a gap-open situation against their position. Usually the first loss is the best loss, and a trader must always use stop-loss orders. This is a lucky exit with the stop placement. Had the position been open with the gap down, then a stop can be placed just below the immediate low of the day to ensure no additional loss is incurred and then the trade can be exited on the first rally. (Refer to Figure 4.15 for stop-loss placement on this trade.) A $2.00 stop-loss would have been used, and the trader would have been stopped out for a loss of $400 on 200 shares.

The use of stop-loss orders is essential in good trading and money management. We never know which trades will win or lose, and controlling the risk allows us to move on to the next trade.

CHAPTER 5

The Gartley "222" Pattern

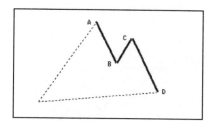

The Gartley "222" pattern is certainly one of the classic retracement patterns. It offers the trader early entry with minimum risk into a potential longer-term trend reversal. For short-term day traders, the pattern can be used effectively to buy and sell tests of highs and lows on an intraday basis. Gartley said to buy or sell the first AB=CD pattern in a new bear or bull market, and that is what this pattern can achieve along with entries into an already established trend. A major reversal may not always follow with this pattern, but even so the trader can still gain profits using good trade management skills (assuming the pattern is not a failure pattern).

HISTORY OF THE GARTLEY "222" PATTERN

The Gartley "222" pattern is named for the page number it is found on in H.M. Gartley's book, *Profits in the Stock Market*. Since then, multiple books have been written describing the Gartley "222" pattern and charting software that applies it. Ensign Software was the first to mathematically provide the pattern in its charting software to be used on any actively traded stock, commodity, or futures market.

Of the almost 500 pages in H.M. Gartley's book, none are more important than pages 221 and 222. This is where the author described this particular pattern in greater detail than any of the other patterns in his book. Gartley referred to it as one of the best trading opportunities. The most revealing part of the Gartley pattern is somewhat hidden on page 222 under Figure 27, which is reproduced here as Figure 5.1.

The greatest challenge with these two pages was trying to interpret the description of this pattern, as it is not as clear as one might expect. Gartley did not give an explanation of this pattern as we use it today. The biggest question that comes to mind is the discrepancy between the two patterns in Figure 27 in Gartley's book. The diagram labeled A shows a simple retracement in a downtrend, but if you look closely at the diagram labeled B, this shows a more complex correction in an uptrend. Diagrams A and B both use the addition of A, B, and C labels that were shown in Gartley's Parallel Trend Lines chart (refer back to Figure 4.1). These distinct differences between the simple and complex

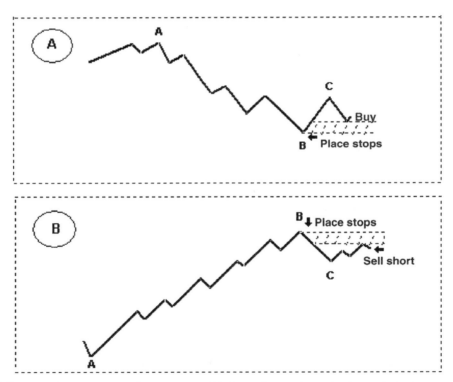

FIGURE 5.1 Reproduction of Figure 27 in *Profits in the Stock Market* by H.M. Gartley.
Source: H.M. Gartley, *Profits in the Stock Market* (Pomeroy, WA: Lambert-Gann Publishing, 1935).

corrections led to the Gartley "222" pattern that we know today. This provided a clearer picture of what the pattern was all about; realizing the differences of the corrections led to a breakthrough after many attempts to understand the concept.

The next step in the development of this pattern was the addition of the mathematical relationships of sacred geometry (which includes the Fibonacci summation series). Adding the Fibonacci ratios to this pattern gave the pattern recognition swing trader the tools to determine price entry, exit points, and stop levels for risk control. The final step was empirically and statistically testing the validity of these patterns. Gartley had emphasized that the pattern was correct approximately 70 percent of the time. Testing weekly, daily, and intraday patterns over the past 40 years has proven that Gartley's original premise was indeed accurate.

GARTLEY "222" PATTERN DESCRIPTION

While Gartley described both buy and sell patterns identically, he had different diagrams for each. It was the AB=CD pattern within the Gartley sell pattern that led to the nickname Gartley "222." Gartley applied this particular pattern to all the market indexes, and he also published it in his weekly newsletter.

The difference between Figure 5.1 (Figure 27 in *Profits in the Stock Market* by H.M. Gartley) and the Gartley "222" pattern that we use today is in the combination of two of Gartley's patterns:

1. The practical use of trend lines diagram from page 249 of Gartley's book (Figure 4.1).
2. Gartley's retracement pattern coupled with the AB=CD pattern (Figure 5.1).

Combining both of these elements creates a buy pattern and a sell pattern.

Larry Pesavento found about 20 years ago that by further adding the ratios from the Fibonacci summation series, he could develop a solid trading pattern. Gartley also used ratios of one-third and two-thirds with this pattern but did not use ratios from the Fibonacci summation series. The main Fibonacci retracement ratios that we apply to the Gartley pattern include: .382 (used with strong trends), .50, .618, and .786. As mentioned in the following section on pattern structure, the 1.00 can be used for a double top or bottom.

Gartley stated in his 1935 masterpiece that over a 30-year period he found these patterns to be profitable in 7 out of 10 cases. The statistics validating this are still the same as Gartley suggested over 70 years ago.

GARTLEY "222" PATTERN STRUCTURE

The structure of the Gartley "222" pattern is almost identical to the AB=CD pattern, with one main difference: It has one added leg that anchors the AB=CD. Whereas the AB=CD pattern is formed with three legs, the Gartley pattern is formed with four legs. The Gartley pattern must contain an AB=CD in order for it to be a valid Gartley pattern. The pattern is labeled from its initiation with an "X." Once this leg is complete, the high or low from "X" begins the AB=CD formation. (See Figure 5.2.)

As with the AB=CD pattern (Chapter 4), the Gartley pattern is also found in all time frames and in all markets. The pattern is a retest of a high or low price and offers the trader an entry into a trade in the direction of the trend. The same rules apply to the AB=CD within the Gartley pattern.

It is important to know what invalidates the Gartley "222" pattern. Here are three items that invalidate the pattern (refer to Figure 5.3).

1. The D completion point cannot exceed X.

2. The C point cannot exceed A. C can be a 1.00 or double top or double bottom of X, though; this is a rare pattern but it is valid.

3. The B point cannot exceed X.

The same warning signs apply to the Gartley pattern as to the AB=CD pattern: gaps in the CD leg near the completion point, wide range bars, and tail closes. (See Chapter 11.)

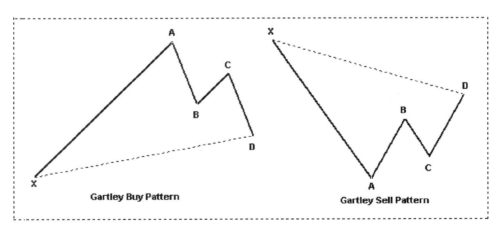

FIGURE 5.2 Examples of the shapes of both buy and sell Gartley "222" patterns with the AB=CD within the Gartley pattern.

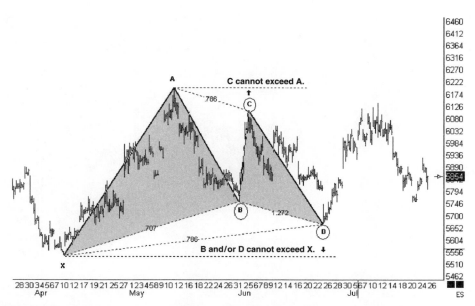

FIGURE 5.3 Soybeans daily chart illustrating the conditions that would invalidate a Gartley buy pattern.

IMPORTANT CHARACTERISTICS OF THE GARTLEY "222" PATTERN

The Gartley pattern can be broken down into four segments that relate to the labeling of the swings. Point X is the high or low point of the swing and is the starting point of the pattern. The X can be found on longer time frames at major highs or lows. However, the X can also sometimes be found as a top or bottom within a larger trend; in other words, the pattern can form within a larger swing or leg without the X being a major top or bottom. (Refer to Figure 5.4.) It is important to remember that most traders will not be initiating trades at exact tops and bottoms the majority of the time, but the Gartley pattern offers the trader a retracement entry into the trend at low-risk trading points and with quantified risk levels.

The X point becomes the fulcrum or anchor price that all technical traders watch daily. After point X is formed and the market begins to move in one direction, the XA leg starts to form; at this stage it is impossible to determine where the completion of the XA leg may be. There are certain characteristics of how this first swing embarks that give clues to the length and thrust of the XA leg: If there are gaps, wide range bars, and tail closes in the direction of the trend, it may be some time before a correction takes place. (Refer back to Figure 4.7.)

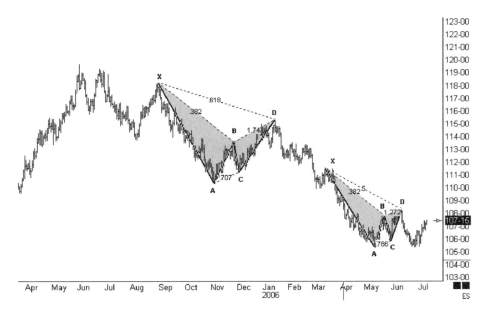

FIGURE 5.4   Daily chart of 30-year bonds showing a good example of a downtrend and the Gartley sell patterns that formed with the X point being within the trend.

As this first leg accelerates, it will take out old support or resistance levels from past chart data. The only way to visually know that the XA leg is complete is by the formation of the second leg, labeled AB. Near the completion of A, many times a doji bar and/or tweezer bar will form, telling us that the momentum may be slowing at this point. A doji bar is a type of Japanese candlestick in which the close is at or near the open of the bar; it is considered a neutral bar. A tweezer top or bottom is also a Japanese candlestick pattern; it forms when two bars have the same high or low. (See Figure 5.5.)

Once it has been determined that the XA leg is complete, then the next step is to watch the formation of the AB leg. This leg is the first reaction up or down from the initial impulse wave from X. The key items to watch in this formation are:

- The Fibonacci retracement ratio to which the market corrects.
- The number of bars that form the leg.
- The similarities in slope and thrust. (See Chapter 4, section titled "Slope and Time Frames.")

For example, if the AB leg takes a considerable amount of time (more than 8 to 10 bars) to form, then we would assume that the market is heading for a larger correction, potentially to .618, .786, or further.

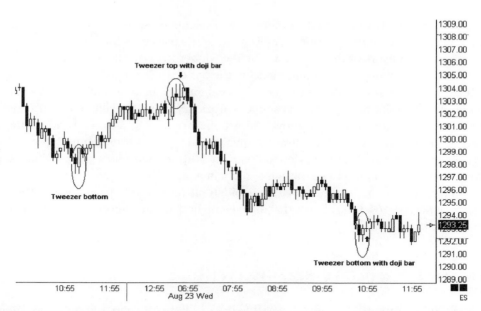

FIGURE 5.5 S&P 5-minute chart showing examples of a tweezer top and tweezer bottom pattern. The tweezer top pattern and the lower tweezer bottom pattern also show a doji bar or a neutral close marked with an arrow.

As the price begins to turn down or up from B, it is important to note that the pattern would be invalid if the BC leg exceeded X. (Refer to Figure 5.3.) It is possible for the completion point of this leg at C to be an exact double bottom or top of the X point, and that is still a valid pattern. But if the price at C exceeds X, the pattern is then invalid; it would potentially be forming a Butterfly Extension pattern. (See Chapter 6 for more on the Butterfly pattern.)

PSYCHOLOGY OF THE GARTLEY "222" PATTERN

In Chapter 4 we described the crowd psychology of the AB=CD pattern. The same elements apply to the Gartley "222" pattern. It is formed by fear and greed levels of the market participants. When the Gartley pattern forms at a major top, the initial move from the top finds support at the A point. (We use a sell pattern as an example here to describe the crowd psychology; refer to Figure 5.4.) Markets rarely go straight up or down without any correction. This point in the pattern is formed when enough market participants view this area as a buying opportunity and the price can rally from there. This is also true from the C point of the pattern. Since there are always buyers and sellers in a market, as the price forms the B and D points, sellers step in, seeing these as areas either to exit the market or to initiate short positions. The D point of the pattern is the moment of truth to determine if the buyers or the sellers will be the winners. A price decline will reward the sellers, and price above the X point will deem the pattern a failure.

If the pattern is successful, the price can accelerate to the downside if it exceeds the A point. At this point many previous support areas are being broken and all traders or market participants who bought above the A point are now at a loss on the positions. It is true to human nature that a few are quick to get out with minimum losses while many others are waiting for the price to come back up to their entry price—which may or may not occur. As the price continues to decline, more market participants who are experiencing larger losses are forced to liquidate at undesirable price levels. There is usually some type of selling climax that signals the bottom, and support is found as new buyers step in.

TRADING THE GARTLEY "222" PATTERN

As mentioned earlier, the Gartley pattern can be found and traded in any time frame. This particular pattern eliminates the need to pick tops and bottoms, as it is a retest of the recent high or low. By definition, it is buying a higher low or selling a lower high, which is ideal for trading with the trend. The trend is defined by higher highs and higher lows in an uptrend and lower highs and lower lows in a downtrend.

The following three trade examples using the Gartley "222" pattern illustrate entry, exit, and stop placements. Refer to Chapter 13, "Building a Trading Plan," to help you develop a personal trading plan for this pattern.

We use two contracts in the futures or commodities trade examples and 200 shares of stock to illustrate scaling out in two parts. We also present a couple of examples under the heading "Alternate Trade Management" to provide an assortment of options for managing these pattern setups.

Trade Setup #1: Gartley "222" Buy Pattern

Market: Soybeans

Contracts: 2

The entry point in this trade is at the .786 completion at point D. See Figure 5.6 for several repetitions of the .786 in this pattern. Notice the second AB=CD pattern that forms within the CD leg, marked in parentheses; this gives us an indication of where the pattern may complete.

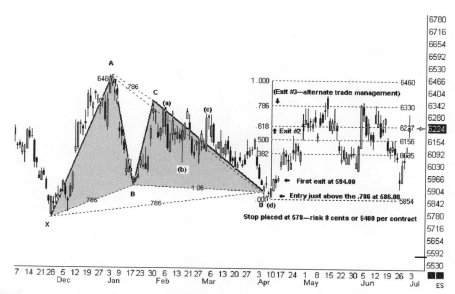

FIGURE 5.6 Soybeans daily chart showing a Gartley "222" buy pattern setup that has three repetitions of the .786 ratio. This may give the trader a clue as to the profit objective.

A limit order just above the .786 at 586.00 would be used on this trade with an initial stop-loss order of 8 cents or $400 per contract. When trading the Gartley pattern it is ideal to be able to place a stop just below the 1.00 (X) level, but this will sometimes be too large for the amount of dollars risked and a dollar amount will be calculated for the stop-loss order instead. Always look at the amount of risk and where the stop must be placed in any trade. If the trader cannot find an acceptable stop level according to the trader's money management plan, then the trade should be dropped and another trade with acceptable risk should be found. We can always reenter a trade that is stopped out if the pattern is still intact. These are the types of decisions that traders must make continually.

Risk-Free Trade   The first exit in this trade at 594.00 will be at a profit of 8 cents or $400. The reason for this is if we risked 8 cents and we can take a partial profit at 8 cents, we can then move our stop up to breakeven and thereby either reduce the risk in the trade or put ourselves in a risk-free trade.

The second exit in this trade is at the .618 at 622.00. This particular trade would have netted +8 cents on the first contract and +36 cents on the second contract for a total of +44 cents per contract, which equals $2,200.

As the price moves in the trader's favor and in the anticipated direction, the trader can trail the stop to lock in profits. There is no exact way to do this, and there is no 100

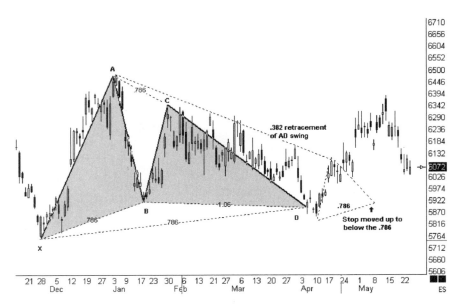

FIGURE 5.7 Soybeans daily chart showing an example of using Fibonacci retracement levels to trail a stop.

percent method that will work all of the time. If the trader is stopped out on a trailing stop prematurely before the price reaches the final profit objective, the trader can reenter the trade on a retracement type pattern (refer to Chapter 8 for more information on retracement entries). A trailing stop may be used by implementing a specific dollar amount or a percentage of price, or by using Fibonacci retracement levels. Place the stop above or below key levels or other visual support or resistance chart levels.

In Figure 5.7 you can see that once the price makes the .382 retracement from the AD swing of the Gartley buy pattern, a new retracement projection can then be done from the most recent swing low price to the high or the swing price at the .382 retracement of the AD leg, and a trailing stop can be placed below the .786 of that retracement. The assumption is that if the price goes below the .786 on that retracement the pattern may be failing. In this case this would have been the third stop placement for this trade:

1. Initial stop at 578.00.
2. Stop moved to breakeven after exit #1.
3. Trailing stop moved to below the .786 retracement.

Alternate Trade Management   In this example we show you exiting in three parts versus two parts. On longer time frames and with larger targets, using a trading strategy that employs a three-part scaling-out exit can produce more profits. The downside, of course, is that if the trade is stopped out at a loss, then additional losses will be incurred. The correct money management for the trader's portfolio should always be used and never exceeded to implement this strategy. Another downside to this strategy is that if the third objective is not reached and the price reverses, the trader may end up giving back some of the profits if the third contract is stopped out below the second profit objective area.

In Figure 5.6 we have marked the .786 level as the third and final profit objective exit. The trader in this particular trade would most likely have been able to gain an additional 11 cents per contract or $550.

Trade Setup #2: Gartley "222" Sell Pattern

Market: Google (GOOG) Stock

Shares: 200

A limit order to sell (refer to Figure 5.8) would be placed just below the .786 at $384.25 per share to sell short. Once the order is filled, immediately place a protective

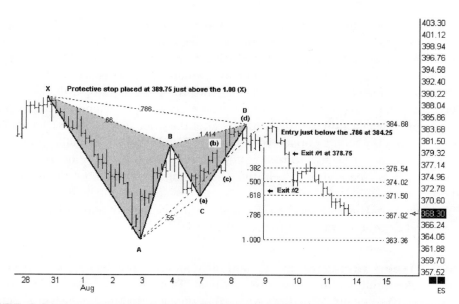

FIGURE 5.8 Google (GOOG) 60-minute chart of Gartley "222" sell pattern. The risk in this pattern is acceptable to place the stop above the X point; the risk is $5.50 per share, very low risk on a $384 stock.

FIGURE 5.9 Google (GOOG) 15-minute chart showing example of dropping down a time frame to help the trader trail stops using most recent swings.

buy stop order above the 1.00 or X level for a risk of $5.50 per share at $389.75. The first profit objective (exit #1) is equal to the amount of risk in the trade at $378.75. Once this is filled, move the stop down to breakeven. Exit #2 is at the .618 at $371.50. We would want to shade the exit order to ensure a fill and would place the order at $371.75. Once the second profit objective (exit #2) is reached, the protective buy stop order is canceled.

Because of the high price of this stock and larger dollar movement, the trader would certainly want to trail a stop to protect profits after the price moves in the trader's favor following moving the stop to breakeven. It can be helpful to use a smaller time frame to see the most recent swings to trail a stop if using visual chart points or Fibonacci retracement levels (see Figure 5.9). In this case, using a 30-minute or 15-minute chart would be sufficient.

This trade would have netted +$5.50 per share on the first exit and +$12.50 per share on the second exit for a total of +$18.00 on the trade.

Alternate Trade Management   An alternate and acceptable way to manage this trade is to take a full exit at the .618 retracement. This would give the trader close to a 3:1 risk/reward trade-off. Why don't we do that on each trade? The answer is simple: We have found over time that taking partial profits around or close to the amount risked gives us a high win/loss ratio on trades and quickly reduces the risk in the trade to close

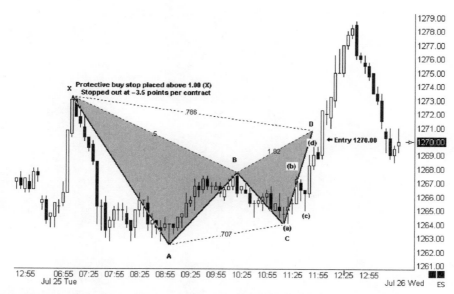

FIGURE 5.10 S&P E-mini 5-minute chart of failed Gartley "222" pattern. A wide range bar, one of the warning signs, is present at the completion point, but it is not likely that it would have been seen in full prior to being filled on the trade.

to a risk-free trade. Whenever we can put ourselves in the position of a risk-free trade we do so.

Trade Setup #3: Failed Gartley "222" Pattern

Market: S&P 500 E-Mini

Contracts: 2

In Figure 5.10, a limit order of 1270.00 to sell short is placed for this trade. A protective buy stop-loss order above the 1.00 (X) point at 1273.50 is immediately placed upon being filled. We would have been filled on this trade before the long bar was complete near the D completion point, which is one of the warning signs. This just happens occasionally and is part of trading. The protective buy stop-loss order keeps this loss small and enables us to move on to the next trade.

Accept the responsibility for the trade regardless of the outcome; this is learning to think in probabilities. The Gartley "222" pattern places a positive expectation in the trader's favor. It is the trader's responsibility to accept the risk, use sound money management, and develop good execution skills.

CHAPTER 6

The Butterfly Pattern

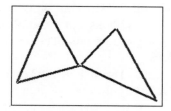

The Butterfly pattern is certainly one of our favorite extension patterns. This particular setup is one that attempts to trade highs and lows at market reversal points. The formations and completions tend to occur at major tops and bottoms, and they can also be seen on all time frames. It is not uncommon to see more than one Butterfly pattern on multiple time frames completing at the same price area.

The risk/reward profile is very favorable with this pattern. The best patterns tend to turn immediately at or near the completion point. It is one of the few patterns that can truly find tops and bottoms. This pattern is not 100 percent, though, and stop-loss orders must be used; as you will see in the last trade setup in this chapter, when this one fails it usually fails in a big way.

HISTORY OF THE BUTTERFLY PATTERN

In order to explain the history of the Butterfly pattern, we have to introduce the Australian trader and developer of the Wave Trader Program, Bryce Gilmore. Bryce has spent a lifetime studying the works of the great masters—R.N. Elliott, W.D. Gann, and many others. He developed the Wave Trader Program in 1988; it was the first computer program to use all the numbers of sacred geometry, including the Fibonacci summation series. This pioneering led to the discovery of the Butterfly pattern.

The Wave Trader Program calculated each swing and ratio and went through a sequence of analyzing that labeled the patterns from 1 to 10, 10 being the level at which 10 swings and ratios came together at the same time and price. This was the level when multiple patterns had completed with the ratios from sacred geometry. Bryce included all the numbers from sacred geometry so that no stone was left unturned. As with many patterns, when the Wave 10 level trades failed it was usually an indication that the market would continue in the direction of the original trend.

Bryce was a perfectionist in everything he attempted. On one occasion he had done extensive analysis on the Treasury bond market and had concluded that T-bonds would not exceed 101.00. He sold T-bonds at 101.00 and used a stop-loss order at 101.02, which is exactly $62.50 per contract. When Larry suggested that the stop might be a bit too close, Bryce shouted, "If those bonds trade above 101.02, everything I've researched, read, and believe in will be a total loss!" He went on to say that if bonds were to trade above 101.03, he would burn all of his books and materials and return to race-car driving and playing golf in his home country of Australia. The bonds made a swing high at 101.00 that lasted more than two months.

The Butterfly pattern came into existence in 1992 on a trading day when Larry was sitting with Bryce watching a Wave 10 pattern form. It appeared in many different colors, and as two colorful right triangles came together Larry commented that it looked like a butterfly. Bryce replied that it was as good a name for the pattern as any, and that is how the name was coined for this pattern. (See Figure 6.1.)

Almost two decades and thousands of Butterfly patterns later, it can be said that it is one of the most profitable trading patterns with the proper use of stop-loss orders. As you go through this chapter and learn this pattern, pay special attention to risk.

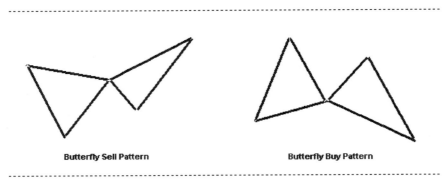

Butterfly Sell Pattern   Butterfly Buy Pattern

FIGURE 6.1 Line drawings of the Butterfly buy and sell patterns showing two connecting triangles.

BUTTERFLY PATTERN DESCRIPTION

The Butterfly pattern is best described as an extension pattern. It is also a failed Gartley pattern where the D completion point completes above the X. Remember that a Gartley pattern is considered a failed pattern if this occurs, but with this failure a Butterfly pattern may be forming. (Refer to Figure 6.2.) The extension of the AD swing and the CD leg can be thought of as a stretched rubber band. It is at these points that the market becomes overbought or oversold and a reversal can occur.

Even if a full reversal does not take place, the trader can still profit on this pattern by exiting on retracements of the CD leg or the AD swing. You will see an example of this in the "Trading the Butterfly Pattern" section of this chapter under "Trade Setup #2." The pattern is formed by two right triangles coming together at one point. It is this formation that gives the pattern its appearance as a Butterfly. The completion points can be calculated by using Fibonacci ratios above 1.00, such as 1.272, 1.618, 2.00, and 2.618. Beyond 2.618 the pattern is considered negated and the trend most likely will continue. In most cases the maximum risk is at the 1.618 level.

Because of the chance that any pattern can be a failed pattern and even the Butterfly pattern can fail, we will note again here that this particular pattern when failed can move

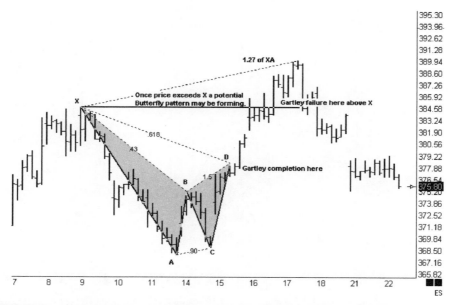

FIGURE 6.2 Google (GOOG) 60-minute chart showing a failed Gartley "222" pattern forming a Butterfly pattern.

very quickly against the trader's position; if the trader does not have the trading skills or discipline to use stops, it is best to not trade this pattern until both of those elements are part of the trader's tool kit.

BUTTERFLY PATTERN STRUCTURE

The Butterfly pattern should be a very symmetrical pattern in its formation and structure. As with the Gartley "222" pattern, the Butterfly pattern is formed with four legs. The difference is that the last leg (the CD leg) of the Butterfly pattern will extend beyond the X point and will move toward the 1.272 or 1.618 expansion of XA. (See Figure 6.3 for an example.) The BC leg will also be an extension, but the completion point is generally determined by the XA swing.

The AB leg of the pattern will usually be at the .618 or the .786 retracement levels. The pattern also is valid if this retracement is at the .382 or .50. This retracement of the AB leg can go further than the .786, as is seen in Figure 6.3, but the pattern will be negated if it goes beyond X. One clue that a Butterfly pattern may be forming is if the first retracement, the AB, goes to the .786 retracement level or further.

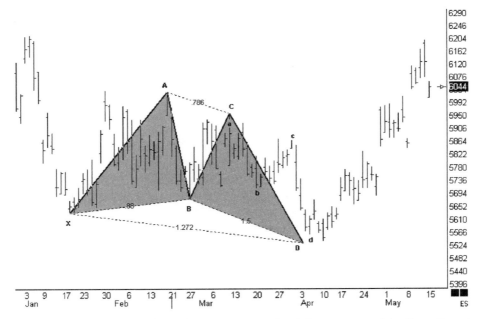

FIGURE 6.3 Soybeans daily chart showing an example of the structure of the Butterfly pattern.

It is important to know what invalidates this pattern; here are five items that would negate this pattern:

1. Absence of an AB=CD within the AD swing. This pattern must contain an AB=CD.
2. An extension move beyond the 2.618 of XA. The 1.618 expansion is generally the maximum risk.
3. B point above (for a sell pattern) or below the X point (for a buy pattern).
4. C above or below the A point.
5. Failure of D to extend beyond X: D must extend beyond X to be a Butterfly pattern.

It is not unusual to see smaller "ab=cd" patterns within one of the main legs; for example, a small ab=cd may be seen within the larger AB=CD formation of the AD swing in Figure 6.3.

Some of our favorite setups are those that contain multiple patterns in several time frames completing in one price area. For more information, see Chapter 8, "Retracement Entries and Multiple Time Frames."

IMPORTANT CHARACTERISTICS OF THE BUTTERFLY PATTERN

This pattern, of all the patterns in this book, can be the most rewarding one if it is indeed a major turning point in a market. It is the ultimate contrarian's trading pattern. The risk, however, can be great if the trader does not take the time to study and learn how to properly assess and manage this pattern. There are several characteristics that should be studied when learning this pattern that will help the trader to identify acceptable risk-to-reward setups and valid patterns. Refer back to Chapter 4, "The AB=CD Pattern," and review the "CD Leg Variations" and "Slope and Time Frames" sections. That information also pertains to the AB=CD within the Butterfly pattern.

Here are three points that are important characteristics of the Butterfly pattern:

1. *Thrust.* How the move from the C point starts is important to watch as it will give the trader information on whether the pattern may form a Butterfly pattern rather than a Gartley pattern—that is, long bars or gaps through the .618 or .786. Gaps should be watched closely by the trader. They indicate an unknown or a change in sentiment and potentially signal changing market conditions. The thrust coming out of the CD leg strongly suggest that the extension has a higher probability of making a 1.618 new high versus a 1.272 new high.

2. *Symmetry.* Study the symmetry of the AB=CD; note the slope and angle of the AB leg and then the CD leg. If the CD leg is exhibiting a steeper angle, that may be a clue that the CD leg will extend beyond X and form a Butterfly pattern. The symmetry or slope of the AB leg should be very close to that of the CD leg in order to keep the ideal symmetry in the pattern. Note also the time bar relationship in these legs; for instance, if the AB leg has taken eight bars to form, then the CD leg should also take approximately eight bars to form, thus forming an ideal Butterfly pattern.

3. *Failure signs.* Beware of price beyond the 1.618 expansion of XA. Generally a move beyond the 1.618 will indicate a continuation of the trend. If the technician will keep focused on these characteristics, it will greatly reduce the potential for getting into trouble with the Butterfly pattern. Butterfly trades are not for the faint of heart, as they enter counter to the trend in markets when they appear the most bullish and the most bearish.

PSYCHOLOGY OF THE BUTTERFLY PATTERN

We have discussed previously in Chapter 4, "The AB=CD Pattern," and Chapter 5, "The Gartley '222' Pattern," how these patterns are formed by basic fear and greed. When there are more buyers, the price rises; when there are more sellers, the price declines. Since the Butterfly pattern is an extension pattern, is found for the most part at major tops and bottoms, and often signals a major reversal point, then we can apply basic mass crowd psychology and witness it at extremes. When this pattern is a major reversal turning point in a market, what you will witness is a market turn and masses heading for the door at the same time. It is an extreme in market emotions of fear and greed.

At the tops, market participants start heading for the door trying to sell. There is fear of losing money on wrong or early short positions, fear of losing profits, profit taking on longs, or initiating new short positions. At the bottoms, market participants start buying perceived bargain prices; others are still heading for the door selling out losing long positions (this has been called the puke point, the point at which traders or investors can not hang on to a losing position one more cent); still others are taking profits on short positions. At this point, any new shorts will be forced to cover losses as prices rise against them, adding more momentum. This point is an extreme of fear of losing or missing out.

At these major turning points, one might notice an unusual amount of press coverage on television and in magazines and newspapers, as well as talk at social gatherings and even randomly on the street or in other public places. All of this coverage or talk will be either very bullish at the top with the Butterfly sell pattern or very bearish at the bottom with the Butterfly buy pattern. The news at this point will be so overwhelmingly skewed in the direction of the trend that it would be difficult to find anyone who would admit to taking the other side of the public viewpoint and opinions. Anyone using long-term moving averages would be nowhere near a decision on taking a countertrend position as the Butterfly pattern nears completion.

Traders should remember that very few traders ever buy the exact high or low of a stock or market and that the Butterfly pattern turns as the last bull buys at the top or the last bear sells at the bottom.

TRADING THE BUTTERFLY PATTERN

The Butterfly pattern can provide instant gratification when the market turns quickly at or near the completion point. However, it can also be one of the fastest loss trades, because the trader is attempting to pick a high or low spot in the market, and if it fails and the trend continues, the trade is usually stopped out quickly. We have stressed several times the necessity of using protective stop-loss orders, and it is especially important with this pattern; this is not a pattern that traders would ever want to let go against them beyond their trading plan and money management plan.

We give three trade examples here and several variations on managing the trades with this pattern.

Trade Setup #1: Butterfly Buy Pattern

Market: Pfizer (PFE) Stock

Shares: 200

(See "Alternate Trade Management" for using a three-part scale-out with the Butterfly pattern.)

This Butterfly buy pattern completes at the 1.272 and has a strong reversal from this point (see Figure 6.4). It is important to note that the gaps and wide range bars are to the advantage of the trader going long on the completion of this Butterfly pattern. This should be a signal that higher prices are likely to come.

The entry point into this trade is at 20.30, with a stop placed below the estimated 1.618 range of XA at 19.50. The stop-loss placement would be at 19.10 for a risk of $1.20 per share or $240 on 200 shares.

When trading any pattern, the risk in the trade must always be acceptable. If it is not, the trader must pass on the trade and find a setup that is acceptable in terms of risk. When trading the Butterfly pattern, it is important to calculate where the 1.618 level is below the 1.272 and to determine whether placing the protective stop-loss order just above or below this level will be an acceptable risk. If it is, then this is the logical place

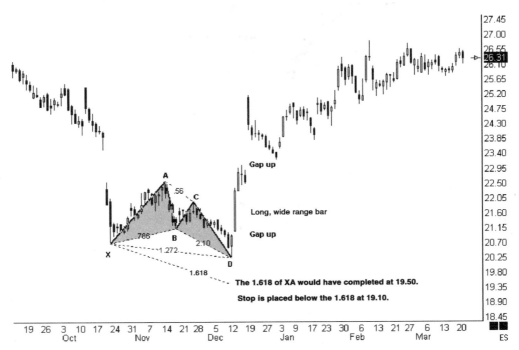

FIGURE 6.4 Pfizer (PFE) daily chart showing a Butterfly buy pattern completing almost to the penny at the 1.272 retracement level. The gaps and wide range bars in this case work to the trader's advantage and should be a signal that higher prices are coming.

to put the stop-loss order. If it is not, then the trader must make a decision to either pass on the trade or possibly enter at or near the 1.618 completion if the price gets there.

Another alternative is to use a dollar amount or percentage of capital for the stop-loss with the knowledge that there may be another entry point at or near that level and to be ready to reenter the trade if stopped out. Still another alternative is to wait for a retracement entry or Gartley pattern to enter the trade. Refer to Chapter 8 on retracement entries and Chapter 5 on the Gartley "222" pattern.

Risk-Free Trade   The first exit on this trade is at the .618 level of the AD swing at 21.70. (See Figure 6.5.) This initial risk in the trade was $1.20 per share, and this exit reduces the risk to just above breakeven. After taking the first exit, the stop-loss order is moved up to breakeven. The stop can be trailed using either a dollar amount, percent of profit the trader feels is the maximum amount to give back, or visual chart points such as the most recent lows or gap areas. The method the trader chooses to trail the stop should be known before entering the trade and should be part of the trade plan.

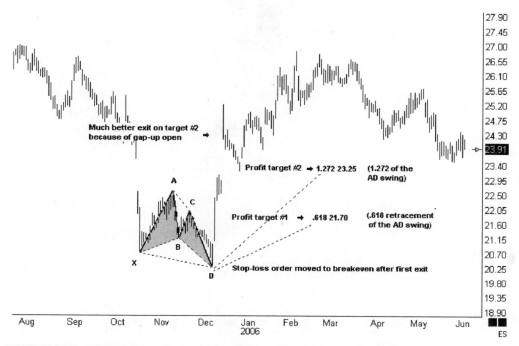

FIGURE 6.5 Pfizer (PFE) daily chart showing Butterfly pattern profit target exits using the .618 retracement level and 1.272 extension.

The second exit in this trade is at the 1.272 extension of the AD swing at 23.25. Sometimes in trading you get lucky, and in this case the market gaps up on the open, exceeding the second target, and would be filled around the opening price at 25.15. This trade would have netted +$625 with an initial risk of $240. Figure 6.5 shows the retracement levels from the AD swing and the first and second exits.

Alternate Trade Management The Butterfly pattern can be managed several ways. The trader's overall market knowledge and experience trading this pattern will determine what method can be used, or traders can develop their own trade management style for this or any other pattern.

We know that when the Butterfly pattern is in full force on a reversal it can be a very powerful move. Because of that, the trader may want to consider devising a trading plan to use a three-part scale-out rather than two when trading the Butterfly pattern. Figure 6.6 shows a retracement from the most recent swing high on the daily chart. An alternate trade management would allow for a first exit at an amount equal to the amount risked on the trade, in this case $1.20. The entry is $20.30 and the first exit would be

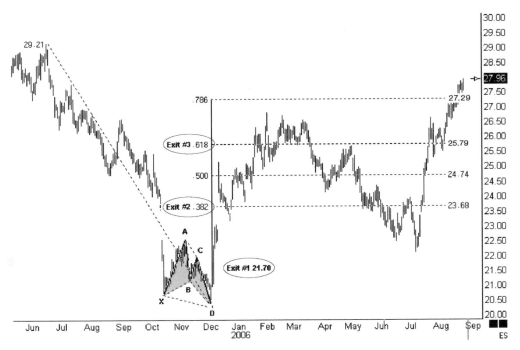

FIGURE 6.6 Pfizer (PFE) daily chart showing alternate trade management using a three-part exit rather than two.

planned at $21.50 with the initial stop-loss order moved to breakeven at that exit. The initial stop remains the same; it does not change with a three-part scale-out. Traders do, however, need to determine whether their money management allows for trading an additional one-third shares. If it does not, then they could divide the number of shares they would trade into three or could stay with a two-part exit plan.

The second profit target using the larger retracement could be taken at the .382. In this example that would be at approximately $23.65, but remember that on this trade the market gapped open higher and the trader would have had a gift from the market with a higher fill at $25.25 on the second exit. Whenever the market offers you a gift—take it!

The stop would then be trailed according to the trader's trading plan, and the third and final exit would be taken at the .618 retracement of the swing. (See Figure 6.6.) You can see from studying the charts of this trade that there are many combinations that can be used. It is best to start with a simple plan based on your skill level and stick with it. As you gain more experience you can adjust your trade management techniques.

Trade Setup #2: Butterfly Sell Pattern

Market: Crude Oil

Contracts: 2

This trade offers a lot for learning the Butterfly pattern and different scenarios that a trader faces daily that require decisions. Take some time to study Figure 6.7 and find all the characteristics within the chart that are noted here:

- There are two Butterfly patterns that formed back to back.
- Butterfly pattern #1 retraced to the .382 of AD of the larger pattern and then continued to new highs. Remember that a .382 retracement can indicate the trend is still intact.
- There is a gap toward the completion point of Butterfly pattern #1.

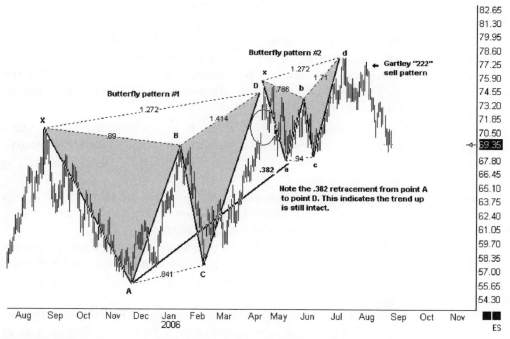

FIGURE 6.7 Study this crude oil daily chart of two Butterfly sell patterns—there is a lot to be learned from it. There is a gap toward the completion point at D of the first pattern, and the similarities of the AB and CD leg are remarkable. The second Butterfly pattern completes at the swing high. There is a Gartley "222" sell pattern following the last high.

- The similarities of the AB and the CD leg in Butterfly pattern #1 are remarkable.
- Butterfly pattern #2 was formed with a double bottom at the a and c points.
- There is a Gartley "222" pattern following the completion of Butterfly pattern #2. The Gartley "222" pattern is a retest and retracement entry into a stock or market. Refer back to Chapter 5 on the Gartley "222" pattern and see Chapter 8 on retracement entries.
- The news at the completion point of both Butterfly patterns was extremely bullish.

The completion point of Butterfly pattern #1 was approximately $74.40, with a shaded entry at $74.35; an initial stop-loss order of $1.00 to $1.50 would be used in a market such as crude oil, which is $1,000 to $1,500 per contract. One of three likely scenarios could have occurred with this setup. The outcome would have been dependent on the size of the stop-loss order used, the decisions the trader would have had to make, and the original trade plan:

1. The trader, if using a $1.00 stop, would have been stopped out at the high of the swing at $75.35 for a loss of $1,000.

2. If a wider stop had been used, $1,500, the trader would have been able to exit the first portion of the trade at an equal risk to the initial stop-loss at $72.85, and would have moved the stop to breakeven and been stopped out on the second half of the trade. This would have netted +1,500.00 on a Butterfly pattern that continued in the direction of the uptrend.

3. Had the trader with a wider stop had the patience to keep the initial stop-loss order in place and exited at the .382 retracement, this strategy would have netted approximately $6.00 per contract or $6,000.

This trade setup is an excellent example of trade management variances. The best thing to do is to have a well-written trading plan and then trade that plan. There will be times when you have outcomes from each of the three scenarios.

Regardless of the outcome of the first Butterfly pattern, a second Butterfly pattern formed, offering another short entry into this market. (See Figure 6.8.) The entry point of Butterfly pattern #2 was at $77.50 with an initial stop-loss order placed at $78.50 for an initial risk of $1,000 per contract.

The first exit in this setup would be at the .382 retracement of CD; remember, this is a double bottom Butterfly pattern, so it makes no difference in this case if the retracement is done from AD or CD, at around 74.50. The market at this point has the earmarks of being at a potential reversal point and therefore has the potential to be a larger win with a relative small risk per contract. The stop-loss order is moved to breakeven upon completion of the first profit target. The second profit target will be at the .618 retracement

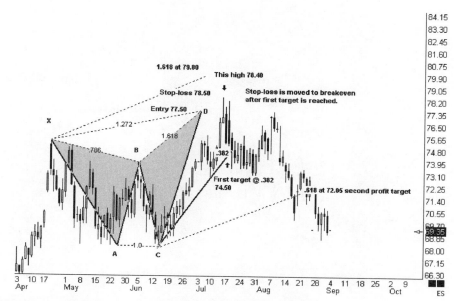

FIGURE 6.8 Crude oil daily chart of Butterfly sell pattern #2.

of CD around 72.05. If the trade is being exited in three parts, the trader would then trail the stop for a potential larger profit exit on the third contract.

The net on two contracts would be $8.45 or $8,450, with an initial risk of $1,000. You can see why it is important for the trader to stay with the trade and trade all the Butterfly patterns that form. We have no way of knowing which ones will work.

Trade Setup #3: Failed Butterfly Pattern

Market: Euro Futures

Contracts: 2

This trade in the euro market was a failed pattern and trade. Look closely at Figure 6.9 and note the AB=CD patterns that formed within the AD leg. We have marked in three of them but there are actually four in total; the chart would be too difficult to read with the last one marked in. You can see how one pattern ends and another begins.

The entry would be 1.2495 with a $500 stop-loss per contract, which is $12.50 per tick (pip) and is placed at 1.2545. Placing the stop just beyond the 1.618 would mean far too much risk for this trade. The bar following the entry is a wide range bar, and this trade would be stopped out in minutes. When Butterfly patterns fail, they generally do

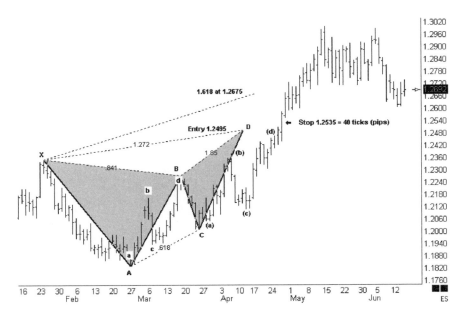

FIGURE 6.9 Euro daily chart of failed Butterfly sell pattern.

so quickly, because when they fail it indicates the trend is still intact and the momentum is still in that direction. A second loss would have been incurred had another trade been entered at the 1.618.

The high of that swing is at approximately 1.3000, which in terms of loss would equate to around 5 full points or $6,250 per contract.

We have been advocating the use of protective stop-loss orders with all of the patterns presented in this book, and especially one as powerful as the Butterfly pattern. It is powerful both in potential gains and in potential losses. Learn to protect your working capital so that you can come back and trade another day.

CHAPTER 7

The Three Drives Pattern

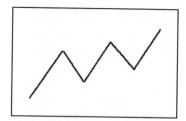

O ne important element that is consistent with all of the patterns in this book is symmetry. Each pattern is symmetrical in its structure. We presented and discussed symmetry with the AB=CD pattern, the Gartley "222" pattern, and the Butterfly pattern. The Three Drives pattern is no exception. Symmetry is at the core of this great trading pattern, as you will learn in this chapter.

HISTORY OF THE THREE DRIVES PATTERN

There is very little written about the Three Drives pattern in pattern recognition books. Most likely the first mention of anything resembling this pattern was by a man named George Cole. Although Cole did allude to the pattern in his book written in 1936, *Keys to Speculation,* he did not accurately describe the pattern. H.M. Gartley came closer than anyone else describing this pattern with his description of the Expanding Five Wave Triangle in *Profits in the Stock Market.* J. Welles Wilder, a popular author on trading in the 1930s, sold Gartley's Expanding Five Wave Triangle as a trading system called the Reverse Point Wave for $2,500.

It wasn't until the 1950s that William Dunnigan, a stock investor from Santa Barbara, California, wrote pamphlets on two trading systems, one titled *The Dunnigan One Way Method*, and the second titled *The Dunnigan Thrust Method*. These two pamphlets were written as the U.S. stock market was evolving into one of the most prestigious financial instruments in the world. This was at a time when investors were still regaining confidence many years after the crash of 1929. Dunnigan did call this pattern Three Drives, and it is likely that he was the first to name this pattern.

John Hill from *Futures Truth*, a publication dedicated to honesty in the futures business, brought this pattern to Larry's attention as a mentor and friend in the 1970s. It is a good trading pattern, although it does not appear on all time frames as frequently as other trading patterns.

THREE DRIVES PATTERN DESCRIPTION

The Three Drives pattern is simple in its structure and should be easy to visually identify on a chart in any time frame. It consists of three evenly spaced tops in an uptrend or three evenly spaced bottoms in a downtrend. The Three Drives pattern also contains an AB=CD. (See Figure 7.1.) It is generally found at tops or bottoms and is the final push up or down before a reversal takes place. It should also be noted that the pattern does not always signal a major reversal—it may be the end of a swing in the trend and a correction will take place rather than a full reversal. If it is a correction, it is likely that an AB=CD pattern or retracement pattern will form following the third drive.

It is important to watch the reaction of the correction pattern for clues. If the correction pattern fails, then the trader may suspect the trend is over. It is not uncommon with reversals to see very sharp moves up or down from this pattern. Refer to trade setup #1 later in the chapter for an example of a correction pattern and trade setup #2 for a reversal from the completion of the Three Drives pattern.

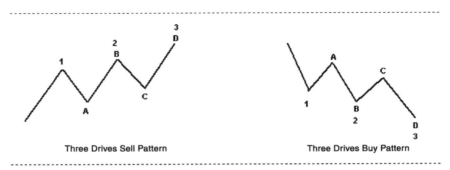

FIGURE 7.1 The Three Drives pattern.

THREE DRIVES PATTERN STRUCTURE

The drives (tops and bottoms) of the pattern are numbered 1, 2, and 3. Each drive is consecutively higher or lower than the last—consecutively higher in a Three Drives to the top pattern and consecutively lower in a Three Drives to the bottom pattern. (Refer back to Figure 7.1.) The distance from the top or bottom of drive 1 to the top or bottom of drive 2 should be a 1.272 or 1.618 extension, and it is the same for the top or bottom of drive 2 to drive 3. It is important to remember that the market may fall a bit short of these levels or may go just a bit farther. The important thing is to watch for a symmetrical pattern to form. There may also be an extension number of 1.272 or 1.618 measuring from drive 1 to A and completing at drive 3. Refer to Figure 7.2 below for an example.

The retracements at points A and C, which form the AB=CD, should be a Fibonacci retracement, ideally at the .618 or the .786. If a retracement at the .382 is formed, it is again a sign of a strong trend. These drives should appear symmetrical to the eye and jump out. If the trader has to force the pattern, it is probably not a Three Drives pattern.

There should also be time symmetry from point A to drive 2 and from point C to drive 3, in that it should take each of these legs approximately the same number of time bars to form.

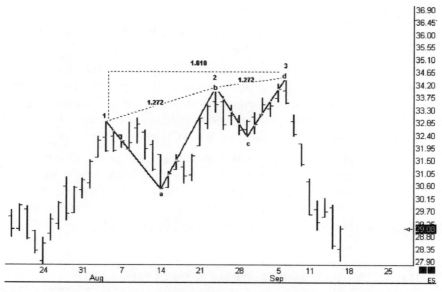

FIGURE 7.2 Barrick Gold Corporation (ABX) daily chart of Three Drives sell pattern. The distance from the top of drive 1 to drive 2 and from drive 2 to drive 3 is a 1.272 extension. The distance from drive 1 to A and completing at drive 3 is a 1.618 extension.

Five items to watch for that would invalidate this pattern are:

1. Drive 1 above or below drive 2 (above in a sell pattern or below in a buy pattern).

2. Drive 2 above or below drive 3 (above in a sell pattern or below in a buy pattern).

3. C below A (for a sell pattern) or above A (for a buy pattern). B should not be above D (for a sell pattern) or below D (for a buy pattern).

4. Extensions that extend past the 1.618 as the Three Drives pattern is forming will usually result in a failed pattern.

5. Large price gaps that appear as this pattern is forming in the direction of the established trend, especially toward the completion of drive 3, are a sign that the pattern is not valid and the trader should wait for further confirmation of a top or bottom or the formation of another pattern.

IMPORTANT CHARACTERISTICS OF THE THREE DRIVES PATTERN

The Three Drives pattern is similar to the Butterfly pattern in that it is very symmetrical. There are three areas of symmetry to study and learn to identify and trade this pattern successfully.

1. *Price symmetry.* Symmetry of price should be equal in the formation of the legs from A to drive 2 and from C to drive 3.

2. *Time symmetry.* The Three Drives pattern will have near-perfect symmetry where the upswings or downswings consist of close to the same number of time bars. If the time bars are not exactly the same, they should be close to a Fibonacci ratio that can be calculated by dividing the number of time bars in each leg—for example, five time bars in the AB and eight time bars in the CD ($5 \div 8 = .625$).

3. *Visual symmetry.* The pattern should be aesthetically pleasing to the eye. Three Drives patterns that are asymmetrical or that are forced should be viewed with suspicion. By force, we are referring to the market technician trying to force the pattern where it does not exist based on the elements outlined in the pattern structure section of this chapter. If it doesn't look symmetrical, it is probably not valid.

PSYCHOLOGY OF THE THREE DRIVES PATTERN

All patterns are formed by crowd psychology, and it is interesting and educational to study what forms any particular pattern. The Three Drives pattern is slightly different in its psychology, as it has three tops or bottoms that must form to complete the pattern, compared to most patterns with one (or occasionally two in the cases of double bottoms and tops).

It is a natural phenomenon that bulls are the most bullish at the tops of markets and bears the most bearish at the bottom. When this occurs there is typically an unusual amount of news that accompanies these tops and bottoms in favor of the excess bullishness or bearishness.

The Three Drives pattern goes through an extended process of bringing in new buyers or short sellers too early at tops with successive waves and new sellers at lows or new buyers who are too early. The pattern generally makes the final wave as the last buyer has bought at the top and the last seller has sold at the bottom. This is the time when the market will appear absolutely the most bullish or most bearish. The last push up or down to form the last gasp in the market is almost like a game of hot potato, and the market has just passed the last hot potato to the last market participant before it changes direction.

As the market then changes direction, each new low below the latest swing low in an uptrend now has more bulls trapped. Conversely, each new high above the previous swing low has more bears trapped. This in itself can add fuel to a rally or decline. Usually it is not until a new trend is well under way that the news media will also change direction.

TRADING THE THREE DRIVES PATTERN

As we mentioned earlier in this chapter, the Three Drives pattern can be either a reversal or part of a correction in a trend, where the market is pausing before resuming the original direction of the trend.

Trade setup #1 illustrates a Three Drives buy pattern that is a correction in a trend. We use an example in trade setup #2 that is a reversal, and we use a failed Three Drives pattern in trade setup #3. Pay particular attention to the chart in trade setup #3 and notice how a failed pattern that is not labeled is much more difficult to spot on a chart.

Setup #1: Three Drives Buy Pattern

Market: QQQQ Daily

Shares: 200

The completion point on the Three Drives buy pattern shown in Figure 7.3 is at the 1.618 level. This was determined by the previous 1.618 from drive 1 to drive 2, which is

FIGURE 7.3   NASDAQ-100 (QQQQ) daily chart of trade setup #1 is an example of a Three Drives buy pattern being a correction in a downtrend rather than a reversal pattern.

repeated from drive 2 to drive 3. Although the time bars are not the same number, they are close to a Fibonacci ratio with 6 bars in the first leg down of the pattern and 10 bars down in the second leg ($6 \div 10 = .60$).

The risk in this trade is very small because of the completion point at the 1.618. The entry is at 62.25, and a stop can be placed at $2.00 per share at 60.25, just below the recent low.

Risk-Free Trade   The first profit target is equal to the risk at 64.25, and the stop can be moved up to just below the most recent swing low at 60.40. The assumption is that with the stop just below the most recent low, the market would be telling us that this pattern is a failed pattern at that point.

The stop would be trailed on this trade. The trader must keep in mind that this is a daily chart and allow for the market to move up and down, giving it enough room and not trailing the stop too closely. In this case the market does reach the second price objective at the .618. This particular Three Drives pattern turns out to be only a correction, and the market turns down from the .618 and makes new lows. Although this trade is a correction in a downtrend and not a reversal, it achieves a very good profit. It would have netted +$14.75 with very low risk.

Trade Setup #2: Three Drives Sell Pattern

Market: S&P E-mini Daily

Contracts: 3

In this trade example we use a three-part exit that we have used in previous trades. It is always up to the trader according to his trade plan and money management plan how many shares or contracts are traded in any given trade. The nature of this particular setup would be conducive to a three-part exit for a couple of reasons:

1. When the extension patterns are reversal patterns, larger gains can be captured by using extension exits. (See Figure 7.4.)

2. There are multiple patterns forming: two Butterfly sell patterns, multiple AB=CD patterns, and a Three Drives pattern. The trader never knows if there will be a market reversal, but with so many patterns and ratios coming into one completion area it may well be worth the risk for a three-part exit. Refer to Figure 7.5 to see the multiple patterns that form in this chart.

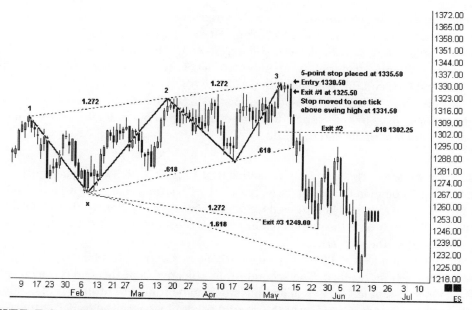

FIGURE 7.4 S&P E-mini daily chart. The Three Drives sell pattern turns out to be a market reversal, and by using a three-part exit strategy the trader is able to capture larger gains. The break of the .618 trend line is a signal to the trader to determine a third profit objective at the 1.272 extension.

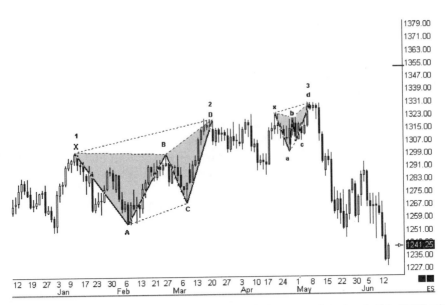

FIGURE 7.5 Multiple patterns are forming and completing around the top in this S&P E-mini daily chart. There are two Butterfly patterns, multiple AB=CD patterns, and a Three Drives sell pattern.

The entry on this sell pattern is at the 1.272 retracement level. Figure 7.4 shows both drives 2 and 3 completing at the 1.272. You can see the natural trend line the market forms with these ratios. Notice also in Figure 7.4 where the .618 retracement level is as the pattern is forming. This will be an important level for the market to break, as it also forms a trend line, and this will signal the trader to try to capture larger gains.

The entry is at 1330.50 with a 5-point stop at 1335.50. Placing the stop above the 1.618 in this trade involves too much risk. If the trade is stopped out, then the trader can look for another entry at or around the 1.618 level.

Risk-Free Trade   The first profit objective is at 1325.50, which would be equal to the initial risk of 5 points in the trade. (See Figure 7.4.) This trade is on a daily chart, and the first profit objective is reached three days after entry. A day trader would exit each day and find a new entry until the market either reached the first profit objective or continued higher, exceeding the stop area.

The initial stop-loss at 1335.50 is moved to one tick above the swing high at 1331.50 once the first exit is reached. The second profit objective is at the .618 retracement at 1302.25. Once this objective is reached the stop can be trailed to protect profits. Figure 7.4 shows a long, wide range bar at the second profit objective. The trader at this point wants to monitor the market for further downside and to determine the best level for the third exit.

The trend line at the .618 retracements that formed the pattern, once broken, gives the trader a profit objective at the 1.272 extension from the point marked X to the top of drive 3. This profit objective is around 1248.25, and the trader should shade the exit to ensure a fill.

This trade on the daily chart would have netted +114.75 points. It certainly is a rare home run trade, and the trader would need to have the patience to let large profits accumulate and reach the price targets and be willing to hold the position overnight, as this particular trade took 13 trading days to reach the third profit objective and exit.

We will revisit this particular pattern again in Chapter 8 on retracement patterns.

Trade Setup #3: Three Drives Failed Sell Pattern

Market: Gold Futures

Contracts: 2

This trade setup (shown in Figure 7.6) is stopped out for a $5.00 loss per contract for a total loss of $1,000. Failed patterns are always more difficult to see, even in hind-

FIGURE 7.6 Gold futures daily chart of Three Drives failed sell pattern. We have said this before, and it is worth repeating looking at this chart: Always honor your stop-loss orders.

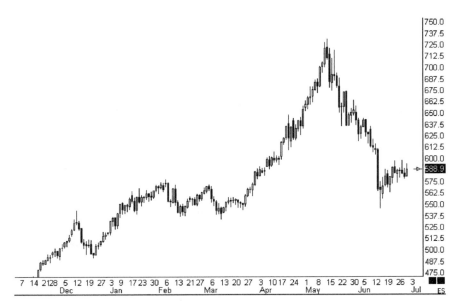

FIGURE 7.7 Gold futures daily chart without Three Drives failed sell pattern drawn in. It is always more difficult to see failed patterns when studying charts.

sight, when you are studying patterns, because they are obscured somewhat by the price movement.

Figure 7.7 shows the same chart with no price pattern drawn in. You can see how difficult it is to find the Three Drives pattern in this chart. The price of gold moves up over $125 per ounce after the failed Three Drives entry; you must always honor your stop-loss orders.

CHAPTER 8

Retracement Entries and Multiple Time Frames

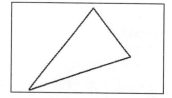

Retracement entries serve several purposes. For example, they can be used if the initial entry point was missed, or they can be used for reentering a trade in the direction of the trend or for adding onto a position.

In this chapter we cover two types of retracement entry patterns that we use in our pattern recognition study:

1. Fibonacci Retracement patterns.
2. Opening Price Retracement patterns.

We have already covered the Gartley "222" pattern in Chapter 5; please review that chapter for using the Gartley "222" pattern as a retracement entry setup. Trend-type retracement entries will be covered in Chapter 10 on trend identification for the S&P 500 market. Retracement patterns are nothing new to the present-day technical analyst, and studying them will add another valuable tool to the trader's market knowledge.

At the end of this chapter we cover the use of multiple time frames, which is a necessary tool for each trader using technical analysis to study and learn.

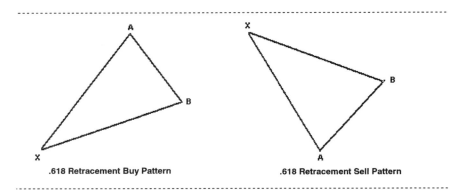

FIGURE 8.1 Examples of Fibonacci Retracement buy and sell patterns. An AB=CD is not present in a Fibonacci Retracement pattern.

FIBONACCI RETRACEMENT ENTRIES

We have covered the AB=CD, Gartley "222," Butterfly, and Three Drives patterns up to this point; all of them are structured with Fibonacci ratios. Fibonacci ratios can be applied and used for retracement entries into a trade as well. The most common Fibonacci retracement ratios used for retracement entries are .382, .50, .618, and .786. These same Fibonacci ratios can also be used for profit objectives and placing stops, as we show in our trade examples in this chapter.

Fibonacci retracement entries differ in one main characteristic from the Gartley pattern in that they do not contain an AB=CD pattern. See Figure 8.1 for diagrams of .618 retracement buy and sell patterns.

FIBONACCI RETRACEMENT PATTERN STRUCTURE

There are only two legs that form a Fibonacci Retracement pattern, as shown in Figure 8.1. The first leg is labeled XA, and the second leg is labeled AB. X is the beginning of the pattern, and B is the completion point. The X generally begins at the high or low of the most recent swing on that time frame, but as with the Gartley pattern a swing in an already established trend may be used. See Figure 8.2 for an example of a long, wide range bar warning sign.

A retracement-type pattern gives the trader an advantage of not having to try to pick a top or a bottom—it is an entry into a trade in the direction of the trend.

As a rule of thumb for analyzing a Fibonacci retracement pattern that does not contain an AB=CD, the number of bars in the two legs that form the pattern can be used

FIGURE 8.2 S&P E-mini 5-minute chart. In this example, the pattern on the right side has a warning sign in the long, wide range bar.

for analysis. Usually, either the trader will see an equal number of bars, such as six bars up, then six bars down (see Figure 8.3 for an example), or the pattern may form as a Fibonacci ratio of the number of bars in the two legs. For example, if the first leg of the pattern consists of eight bars, then the trader would want to see the second leg form with eight bars or form as a Fibonacci ratio of that number, such as five bars. This would create the .382, .618, or .786 retracement in time.

When these time ratios come together with the price ratios, it is what W.D. Gann referred to as the squaring of price and time, which is nothing more than the description of the geometric triangle. Do not get too caught up in exact bar counts; there may be a perfectly acceptable pattern that is very close to the description but not exact. (See Figure 8.4.) You want to use bar counts as a guideline, not absolute. A trader would want to be aware of and alert to seeing something along the lines of the XA forming with 10 bars and then the AB completing with only 2 or 3 bars. This would be a warning sign that there may a stronger shift in emotion that is causing the pattern to complete rapidly, and the trader would then want to wait for either another pattern to form or some type of confirmation before entering that trade.

The warning signs are the same as previously described in Chapters 4 through 7. Please review those chapters for warning signs that would either invalidate the pattern or

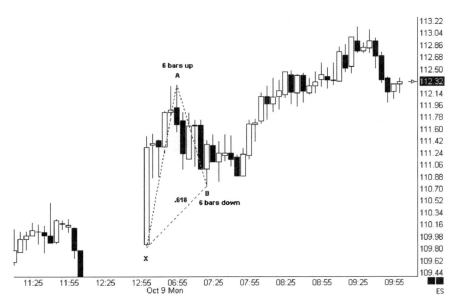

FIGURE 8.3 This 5-minute chart of Research in Motion Limited (RIMM) shows a retracement pattern that forms with six bars up and then six bars down. The completion point is at the .618 retracement.

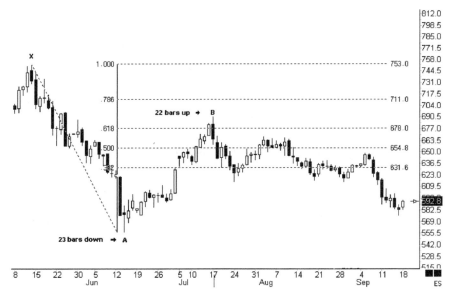

FIGURE 8.4 Gold futures daily chart showing a Fibonacci Retracement pattern with a close, but not exact, time count.

alert the trader to wait for further confirmation. See the "Warning Signs and Confirmation Signs" section of Chapter 11 for more detailed information.

TRADING THE FIBONACCI RETRACEMENT PATTERN

In this section we look at three trade examples using a Fibonacci retracement entry. The first trade example is a Fibonacci Retracement sell pattern, and the second is a buy pattern. These are followed by a failed buy setup.

Trade Setup #1: Retracement Sell Pattern

Market: INTC

Shares: 200

In the trade shown in Figure 8.5, there is a long, wide range bar just before the .618 entry level. This would alert the trader to wait for the .786 or a confirmation that

FIGURE 8.5 This Intel Corporation (INTC) daily chart retracement sell setup is an especially nice trade, with the market helping the trader out with a large gap-down open to the second profit objective.

momentum has slowed. Using the .786 as an entry into this trade, the trader has an excellent risk/reward setup. With the entry at $27.45 and a protective buy stop-loss order placed just above the X point at $28.90, the trade has a total risk of $290 using 200 shares.

Risk-Free Trade   The first exit is at the amount equal to the stop-loss order, which is $1.45 per share. The market reaches the first profit objective within four days. The stop-loss order is then moved down to the breakeven point after exit #1.

The market has a large gap-down open through the .618 retracement from AB and offers the trader an exit at the 1.00 level around $22.55. There is an old saying in the markets: "When the markets offer you a gift—take it."

Alternate Trade Management   We have discussed in previous trade examples alternate trade management suggestions. As an alternative in this case, the trader could at this point, depending on one's risk profile and market experience, choose to trail a stop in an attempt to gain larger profits. If the trader had an order sitting in the market to exit the second part of the trade at the .618 retracement level, he would have been filled on the gapdown open around the opening price that day.

Another consideration and possible alternate form of trade management with these types of conditions is to move the stop-loss order a small amount above the high of the day about 20 to 30 minutes after the open following a large gap such as this. Using this type of trade management would still allow the trader to exit the second portion of the trade with a nice profit if the stock moved up and rallied following the gap-down open, but if the stock then declined further following the gap-down open it would offer the trader an opportunity for larger gains.

Trade Setup #2: Retracement Buy Pattern

Market: QQQQ

Shares: 200

This is an almost picture-perfect setup and trade; if only they could all be just like this! The risk in this trade is very low, placing the stop just below the X point. The entry is at the .618 retracement level at $38.55 with the stop-loss order placed at $37.90 for a total risk of 65 cents a share or $130 for the 200 shares in the trade.

If you study Figure 8.6, you will notice the long bars when the market turns up. This will help us determine a second profit objective. This is also an alert to the trader that the

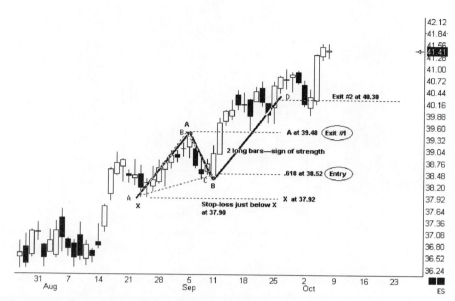

FIGURE 8.6 NASDAQ-100 (QQQQ) daily chart retracement buy setup—a picture-perfect retracement trade.

market may make new highs from this retracement pattern in the direction of the trend, which you can see is up.

Risk-Free Trade   Exit #1 is at $39.45 (the order would be shaded down just a few cents from point A). The stop-loss order can then be moved up to breakeven. The market easily breaks to new highs after the first profit objective is met. We now have a risk-free trade and can let the market move up to the second profit objective. In this case, because of the early signs of upward momentum that we saw in the long bars, we will use the D point of the AB=CD pattern that can be seen forming in Figure 8.6. Exit #2 at this point is at $40.30. This is certainly a profitable trade on a pattern that offered a good entry with low risk.

Alternate Trade Management   Traders' knowledge and market skill at reading market momentum will have an effect on how they manage trades. In the case of this trade, a skilled and experienced trader may well read the signs of market momentum to the upside and trail a stop up on a portion of the trade to try to capture larger gains if offered. As traders gain more experience, their trading skills and ability will improve with time and they will recognize particular instances in the market when it may be prudent to hold for larger gains.

FIGURE 8.7 S&P E-mini 5-minute chart showing failed retracement buy pattern setup.

Trade Setup #3: Retracement Buy Failed Pattern

Market: S&P E-mini

Contracts: 2

The entry in this retracement pattern (see Figure 8.7) is at the .618 level at the price of 1355.50, with the stop-loss order placed just above the X at 1358.25 for a total risk of 2.75 points per contract or $137.50. After the initial entry, the market starts to turn down toward the first price objective but only reaches 1354.50 before turning up and stopping the trade out at a loss. After the trade is stopped out, the market then turns down and comes back close to the initial entry point. There is no way for the trader to anticipate this, and the best way to manage trades for loss control is always through the use of stop-loss orders. These types of occurrences are a part of trading.

OPENING PRICE RETRACEMENT SETUPS

The Opening Price Retracement patterns can be used either for day trading stocks or for originating or adding onto positions using a longer time frame. We use the opening price setups for stocks only and do not use them in other markets. The concept is simple;

the opening price will be near the high or low of the day more than 60 percent of the time—that is, within the upper or lower 20 percent range of that day, according to *The Opening Price Principle* by Larry Pesavento and Peggy MacKay.

The best way to appreciate this setup is to study charts and to note the opening price and where the closing price is in relation to it in a given time frame. The opening price seems to act like a magnet; why this occurs is not fully known. One theory is that traders and investors have had 16 to 18 hours since the previous close to contemplate the next day's orders, and those orders are placed near the open of the next day.

When using the Opening Price Retracement setup, it is important to use only the current day's opening price and to not use the previous day's opening or closing prices; they are irrelevant. This method is a simple concept for day traders, and the risk is easily quantified, as we have seen in our previous retracement trade setups. Simply stated, if the price is above the opening price, the probability of a winning long trade is above 60 percent; conversely, if the price is below the opening price, the probability of a winning short trade is above 60 percent.

MARKET SETUP FOR THE OPENING PRICE RETRACEMENT TRADE

To use the Opening Price Retracement setup, the trader wants to look for specific criteria before initiating a trade. These criteria include:

- A price above or below the opening price of a specific stock 30 to 60 minutes after the open.
- A retracement of .618 or .786 above or below the opening price.
- A setup absent of warning signs. (See Chapter 11.)
- An acceptable stop placement and risk level.

As an example of a long trade using the Opening Price Retracement, a trader would look for a stock that is trading above its opening price 30 to 60 minutes after the open that day and would then look for a .618 or .786 retracement level from the low price off the open to the current high of the day for an entry point. The trader must be able to place an acceptable stop-loss in order to accept the trade. (Refer to Figure 8.8.) The entry at the .618 or .786 retracement level positions the trader in the direction of the opening price with the trade, and the odds for a successful trade are in the trader's favor. The opposite would be true for a short trade; the trader would initiate the trade by selling a .618 or .786 retracement from the high of the day off the open and the current low and would then be positioned in the market in the direction of the opening price.

FIGURE 8.8 Centex Corporation (CTX) 5-minute chart showing long Opening Price Retracement trade setup. Note the long, wide range bar off the open. This makes an ideal setup.

A 5-, 15-, 30-, or even 60-minute time frame could be used—whatever the trader is comfortable with. We will use a 5-minute chart for our trade examples with this setup.

TRADING THE OPENING PRICE RETRACEMENT SETUP

Trade Setup #1: Opening Price Retracement Buy Setup

Stock: CTX

Shares: 200

The long entry on this opening price setup is at the .618 retracement level at $48.25. The stop-loss order is placed just below the low of the day at $47.70 for a total risk of 55 cents per share or $110. In Figure 8.8 illustrating this trade, you can see a long, wide range bar off the open. This is an especially ideal setup; the long, wide range bar is suggesting momentum to the upside, and the retracement entry should offer support at the .618 with very low risk in the trade.

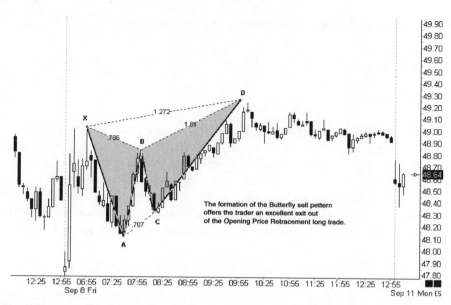

The formation of the Butterfly sell pattern offers the trader an excellent exit out of the Opening Price Retracement long trade.

FIGURE 8.9 Centex Corporation (CTX) 5-minute chart showing Butterfly sell pattern that can help the trader determine the second exit.

Risk-Free Trade The first profit objective is the first .618 retracement from the high of the first swing to the low of the first retracement. In this example, exit #1 is at $48.65 and the stop-loss order is then moved up to the breakeven point. The trader can, if he chooses, move the stop to just below the first swing low of the entry retracement. It should be noted that this trade is a day trade method, and the trader does not want to be in a position to give back profits if at all possible. Moving the stop to breakeven will put the trader in a risk-free position with the potential to gain further profits. You will have to study Figure 8.8 and observe how the trade is managed. When day trading, it is important to obtain a risk-free trade as soon as the market offers it and take profits when available. The best way to do this is by outlining a detailed trading plan and getting into the habit of pulling your stop-loss down as soon as the first profit objective is reached.

See Figure 8.9 for the formation of a Butterfly sell pattern that would help the trader determine the second profit objective. It is also an option, if allowed in the trader's risk management and money management plan, to exit in three stages if one feels that is the best way to manage the trade.

Exit #2 is at the 1.27 extension and completion area of the Butterfly sell pattern at $49.20.

Trade Setup #2: Opening Price Retracement Sell Setup

Stock: GS

Shares: 200

This trade example was chosen to illustrate the importance of trade management and to show that not every Opening Price Retracement trade will be a large winner. This example will also serve as our alternate trade management example.

As in our first opening price example, there are long, wide range bars off the open. The market continues down and then comes back and makes a .618 retracement, offering an entry short into the trade. The entry into this trade is at the .618 retracement at $148.90. The initial stop-loss order is placed just above the high of the day at $149.75 for a total risk on the trade of 85 cents per share or $170.

In Figure 8.10, the price retraces after the entry down to the .382 and .50 retracement levels. It is quite feasible for a day trader to take partial exits at either of these levels and then move the stop-loss order to breakeven. In this particular example a small profit would have been obtained before being stopped out on the balance. There is no way to determine in advance which of the retracement levels the market may turn from, and it

FIGURE 8.10   Goldman Sachs Group (GS) 5-minute chart showing an Opening Price Retracement sell setup that offers a small profit before the trade is stopped out.

is up to the trader to determine the risk in the trade and the profit objectives. It is always good to keep in mind that the day trader is trading for short-term profits and to take those when they are available.

A partial exit at the .382 retracement in this example would have netted a 45-cent profit on a trade that otherwise would have been stopped out for a loss.

Trade Setup #3: Failed Opening Price Retracement Sell Setup

Stock: AA

Shares: 200

This setup has a gap-down open and long, wide range bar, suggesting further downside to come. But as stocks and markets often do, they have a different idea. The entry is at the .618 at $27.35 with the stop-loss at $27.60 for a total risk of 25 cents per share or $50 on 200 shares.

The trade is stopped out at a loss. Notice on the chart in Figure 8.11 how the market after the entry into the trade consolidates sideways rather than moving toward a retracement level; the trader can move the stop closer if he determines that the market is not doing what it is supposed to do within a reasonable amount of time. There is no way for the trader to anticipate this, so it is best to always manage trades for loss control through the use of stop-loss orders. These types of occurrences are a part of trading.

MULTIPLE TIME FRAMES

In this section we discuss using multiple time frames and present several chart examples to illustrate how they can be used. The information that a trader can gather by using multiple time frames is invaluable and can be used to initiate entries into trades, stay on the sidelines when appropriate, and even help in placing stop-loss orders.

Other advantages of using multiple time frames that we cover include:

- Allowing the trader to get a micro view of larger time frames, which can in turn confirm the trader's original analysis of a trade. It is like using a backup pattern and fine-tuning an entry. An example would be having a pattern on a 60-minute chart and using a 5-minute chart to confirm the entry. (See Figures 8.12 through 8.14 an examples.)

FIGURE 8.11 Alcoa (AA) 5-minute chart example of a failed Opening Price Retracement sell setup.

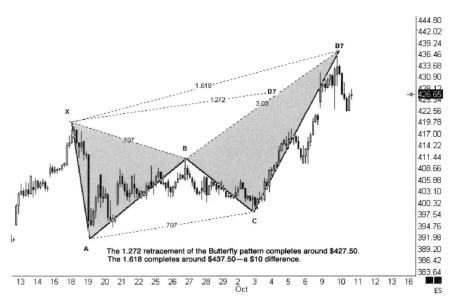

FIGURE 8.12 Google (GOOG) 60-minute chart showing a Butterfly sell pattern that has completed.

- Risk can be managed more effectively by combining time frames. A trader can learn to move stops on smaller time frames for patterns that complete on larger time frames.
- Using multiple time frames from larger to smaller can help the trader to be aware of contrary or opposing patterns that form on smaller time frames that are against the longer-term time frame.

The trader will always want to view larger time frames first for an overall view of the market or stock being studied, and then move down to smaller time frames. Many traders use varying combinations of multiple time frames—weekly charts with daily charts, daily charts with 60-minute charts, 15-minute charts with 5-minute charts, and so on. Some traders use all time frames starting with the largest and scaling down through each time frame to the shortest. It is a matter of preference and experience.

A word of caution: Do not reverse the process by initiating a trade on a short time frame such as a 5-minute chart, planning exits on that time frame, and then moving to daily charts. This is especially true if the trader is at a loss on a trade on a small time frame that is designed as a day trade, and then looks to longer-term charts for signs of a turnaround and tries to turn the trade into a position trade. Position trades should be entered from a position trading plan, and day trades should be entered from a day trading plan.

Managing Risk Using Multiple Time Frame Examples and Fibonacci Retracement Setups

Using Fibonacci Retracement setups with multiple time frames is a natural combination. Many times a trader will come across a pattern that has already completed on a larger time frame and observe that the trade has already moved in the anticipated direction; the trader now needs to find an entry into the trade. Using a Fibonacci retracement level and then scaling down to a smaller time frame is an excellent method for entering a trade in that manner. See Figure 8.12 for a 60-minute Butterfly pattern that forms and is completed on Google stock.

Looking at Figure 8.12, the 1.272 extension of the Butterfly does not hold, and the pattern is completed at the 1.618. Let's take a look now at a 5-minute chart showing the 1.272 price level around $427.50 per share. If the trader had entered there using a lower time frame, he would have been able to manage the risk in the trade with the use of a stop-loss order and then reenter the trade at the 1.618 again using a 5-minute chart. Refer to Figure 8.13 to study the 1.272 price level.

The first thing to notice on this micro view of the 60-minute pattern is that there is a gap-up open and a long, wide range bar. These are both warning signs to alert the trader to either pass on the trade or wait for another acceptable entry. The market during

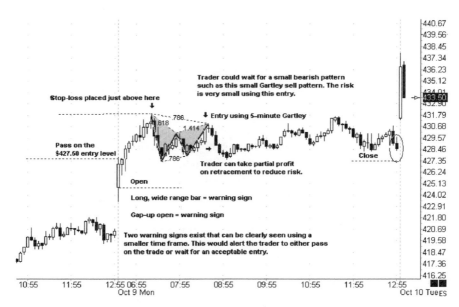

FIGURE 8.13 This Google (GOOG) 5-minute chart shows the 1.272 completion point of the 60-minute Butterfly pattern at $427.50.

the day on the 5-minute chart presents an opportunity for entry by forming a 5-minute Gartley sell pattern. This offers a very low-risk entry into a very high-priced stock. The risk in this trade using this small 5-minute pattern and placing the stop just above the high of the day is around $2.00 per share.

A partial profit could be taken on the retracement of the 5-minute Gartley pattern and the stop kept at the initial location if the trade is being held overnight. This trade would have been stopped out if held until the next morning and would have been a breakeven or very small loss trade.

If the trader then wants to initiate another entry at the 1.618 completion level of the 60-minute Butterfly pattern, the 5-minute chart can be used to aid the trader. See Figure 8.14 for a micro view of the entry using the 1.618.

Many times in trading you have to initiate multiple attempts into a trade in order to achieve a larger gain. It is very important to learn techniques to manage the risk when reentering trades in this manner. In Figure 8.14, GOOG gaps up on the open and has a long, wide range bar. This time the price reverses and trades below the opening price. Once the price forms the 5-minute Gartley sell pattern and Opening Price Retracement sell pattern, it offers an excellent entry into the trade with very little risk. The risk in this trade with the stop-loss placed just above the high of the day is just around $3.00 per share.

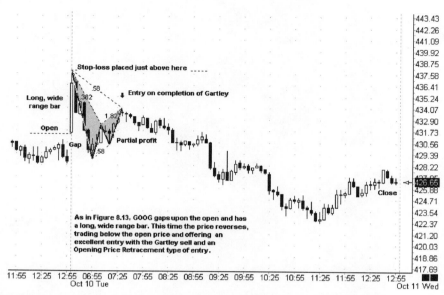

FIGURE 8.14 Micro view of trade entry from the Google (GOOG) 5-minute chart of the 1.618 completion area from the 60-minute Butterfly sell pattern.

The trader can then reduce the risk in the trade and/or put oneself into a risk-free trade by taking partial profits at the .618 retracement level equal to or close to the amount of risk in the trade. If day trading, then the trader would close the trade at the end of the day. If the trader is position trading based on the longer-term 60-minute chart, a stop-loss order would be kept working and the trader would then use larger profit targets based on the 60-minute chart retracements and trail a stop to protect profits.

Multiple Pattern Completions in Multiple Time Frames

Now let's look at an example of multiple patterns in multiple time frames completing around the same price area. Refer to Figure 8.15 and the Gartley "222" sell pattern on the daily time frame. We'll look at Figure 8.16 next for a closer view and another sell pattern that forms and is completed on a 15-minute chart in the same price area.

The high of point D on the daily Gartley "222" sell pattern is at 1.2891 and the 15-minute D completion point is at 1.2888—within a few ticks (pips) of the larger time frame. When there is a congestion area of support or resistance price levels that are formed by multiple patterns, the trader can use that information for entering trades, placing stop-loss orders and profit-taking objectives.

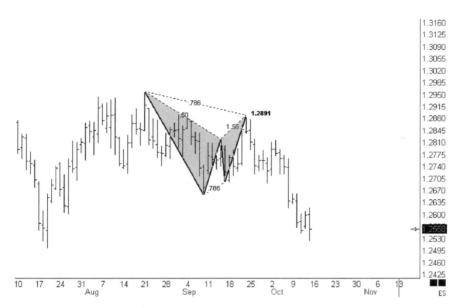

FIGURE 8.15   Daily chart of the euro shows a Gartley "222" sell pattern.

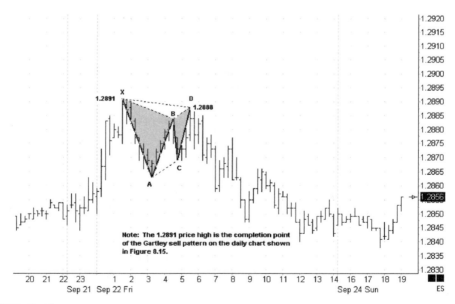

FIGURE 8.16   This chart of the euro shows a 15-minute Gartley "222" sell pattern that completes within a couple of ticks (pips) of the daily Gartley "222" sell pattern in Figure 8.15.

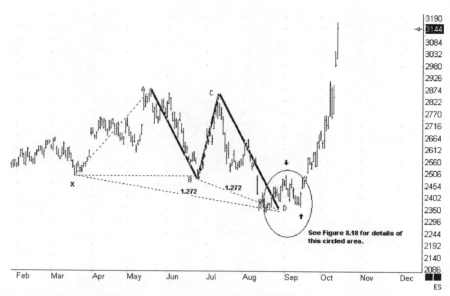

FIGURE 8.17 Corn daily chart shows a large bullish Butterfly pattern and AB=CD pattern completing.

Opposing Patterns on Multiple Time Frames

Our last example in this chapter shows you an example of a daily chart of corn (Figure 8.17) and a 30-minute chart of corn (Figure 8.18) that can be used to alert the trader to opposing price patterns.

The corn daily chart (Figure 8.17) shows a larger Butterfly pattern and AB=CD pattern with a completion point at D. Notice the circled area on this chart. If you look closely, you will see that after the completion of the buy pattern a sell Gartley "222" pattern forms and shortly after that pattern another Gartley "222" buy pattern. Figure 8.18 shows a detail of these two patterns that are clearly visible on the 30-minute chart.

The information offered by these two conflicting patterns can be used in several ways:

- Assuming the trader, after entering the large Butterfly/AB=CD buy pattern, has already taken partial profits and is anticipating a larger move based on the larger time frame pattern, the trader could manage the risk in the trade by observing whether the AB=CD sell pattern makes new lows; if it does, the Butterfly buy pattern would be considered a failed pattern. A stop-loss order at the low of the completion of the daily Butterfly pattern could be maintained at that level, and the trader would be stopped out with a small profit on the trade. Once the trader sees that the Gartley

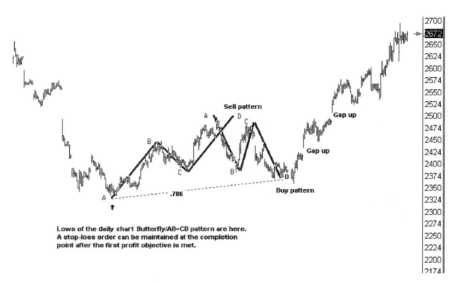

FIGURE 8.18 Corn 30-minute chart shows two opposing Gartley "222" patterns that have formed. One is a Gartley "222" sell pattern and the other is a Gartley "222" buy pattern.

"222" sell pattern failed by making highs above the X point of that pattern, the trader can then move the stop-loss order up to protect profits. Since the trader is working with a larger time frame such as the daily chart in this example, it is important to not move a stop-loss order too close and to give the market enough room to move around, as well as to use the chart points that would suggest a failure of the pattern.

- Another important point for a trader who chooses to trade the Gartley "222" sell pattern in Figure 8.18 to be aware of is that the risk in the trade can be closely managed based on an awareness of a larger time frame pattern that has completed and is thus far profitable. A trader in this situation would want to be cognizant of stop-loss protection and diligent in taking profit objectives.

- The Gartley "222" buy pattern that also formed in the 30-minute time frame gives a trader who missed the original entry point an excellent entry into the trade with a quantifiable risk and stop-loss level using point X of the daily Butterfly/AB=CD pattern.

- A trader could also use the Gartley "222" buy entry to add onto an existing position in the market being traded. Adding onto a position must always be within the trader's trade plan and money management and risk parameters. This type of trading must also be within the trader's skill and market knowledge level.

Notice also in Figure 8.18 the gap up areas on the right side of the chart. These are certainly showing a shift of sentiment in this market, and that information can be used to the advantage of the trader who is long—that higher prices may be ahead and it would be a good idea to hold the position. Conversely, it would give a trader who was short that market an alert to tighten stops or exit the trade.

We have covered several areas using and interpreting information based on multiple time frames. The trader should always be aware of the larger time frames and the overall market conditions of any market or stock one is trading and learn to combine time frames to improve one's trading skills.

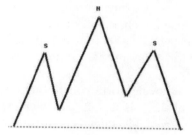

CHAPTER 9

Classical Technical Analysis Patterns

Since the beginnings of technical analysis, classical technical patterns have been repeating over and over in all time frames and in all markets. It's interesting that these patterns have not changed in centuries. They are truly a reflection of crowd psychology. We present three of these classical technical analysis patterns in this chapter and show you how Fibonacci ratios can be applied. Many times you will see the structures of the patterns form with exact Fibonacci ratios. Adding the Fibonacci ratios to these patterns will give the trader an additional tool for timing entries and controlling risk.

We present the Double Top and Double Bottom pattern, the Head and Shoulders pattern, and the Broadening Top and Broadening Bottom pattern. These three patterns were first publicized in R.W. Schabacker's book, *Stock Market Theory and Practice* (B.C. Forbes, 1930). We will take a look at these patterns both from a structural sense of how they are formed and from a trading perspective with ideas for entering the trades, placing stops, and taking advantage of areas to reverse a position. Some of the best trading opportunities can come from failed patterns, and it certainly is true with these patterns when they fail.

A BRIEF HISTORY OF TECHNICAL ANALYSIS

The history of technical analysis using charts to monitor price dates back at least 1,000 years and was first documented by the Japanese. They used rice as a gauge to determine supply and demand. In the late 1800s into the early 1900s an evolutionary process occurred and launched a technical revolution of sorts by great technical analysts such as Jesse Livermore, H.M. Gartley, W.D. Gann, Richard Wyckoff, Richard Schabacker, Ralph Elliott, Charles Dow, George Cole, and a host of others too numerous to mention who devoted their time and lives to the art, science, and skill of technical analysis. An extraordinary note is that much of their work was done by hand. Computers were not available to compute moving averages and instantly call up charts of various time frames with multitudes of indicators and filters applied. These pioneers hand drew their charts meticulously, carefully noting market observations that were then tested and applied as theories and trading strategies. These technicians were great market observers, and today many of the great traders still do some chart work by hand on a daily basis as part of a daily ritual. There were services available that furnished daily or weekly charts of around 50 select individual stocks for a fee, but it certainly was a long way from the real-time data we enjoy today.

Through the Depression years and even World War II, there was very little printed material available regarding technical analysis. The first financial news printed in newspapers, long before the *Wall Street Journal*, had begun about 10 years after the Civil War. As communications advanced and improved, so did the ease of gaining financial information through ticker tape, teletype, and telephone. Some of us can remember using the ticker tapes through the Chicago Board of Trade and the Chicago Mercantile Exchange during the late 1960s and early 1970s.

As the Internet and home computers became accessible, the communications industry as related to financial information and technical analysis programs exploded. Real-time data and charting software packages loaded with every indicator and testing capability imaginable are now available to both the novice technician and the professional alike.

For many years technical analysis was looked at by the financial community as a form of voodoo and not worthy of consideration for seriously making money. Books such as Jack Schwager's *Market Wizards* have dispelled these myths with interviews from some of the greatest traders of our time, like Marty Schwartz, who embrace technical analysis as the core of their trading strategies. In his interview with Schwartz, Schwager asks about his transition from a fundamental to a technical analyst. Schwartz's reply clearly indicates that it was not until he went to technical analysis after using fundamentals for nine years that he became rich.

As we mentioned at the beginning of this chapter, only recently has the academic world given its blessing (through its research) to the validity of technical analysis and the repetition of particular patterns that make it possible for traders to profit.

BASICS OF TECHNICAL ANALYSIS

Everything in technical analysis starts with a single bar chart. This bar chart is plotted on an x-axis and y-axis showing time and price. The price bar represents the total sum of all buyers and sellers for that bar in that time frame. The individual price bars give a great deal of information:

- The high price of the bar.
- The low price of the bar.
- The opening price of the bar.
- The closing price of the bar.
- The time frame of the bar.

Volume is also involved in the formation of the bar. The reason a bar forms is irrelevant; what is important is how multiple bars form in relation to one another over a period of time to create particular patterns that repeat. It is important that the technical analyst learn to read these bars as patterns and act appropriately when a pattern forms that offers a trading opportunity.

DOUBLE BOTTOM AND TOP PATTERNS

R.W. Schabacker stated that the Double Bottom pattern was an important chart formation. This pattern can be found at major bear market bottoms and is a reversal pattern and an accumulation phase. The Double Top pattern is just the opposite; it is a reversal pattern and a distribution phase and can be found at major tops. The pattern may also form as an intermediate pattern in a longer trend that is established.

Double Top and Bottom patterns are seen with a fair amount of regularity on price charts in all time frames. They are sometimes referred to as W bottoms because of the apparent shape forming the letter W. It is probably one of the most common patterns that novice technical analysts become aware of. As a reversal pattern it can be very powerful. If the pattern is seen on an index chart, then it is probable that the same pattern will be forming on many stocks that are in that index.

Double Bottom Pattern Example

If you will take a moment to examine Figure 9.1 and the example of the Double Bottom pattern on the Dow Index, you will see long, wide range bars to the downside that are indicated with arrows. They generally would indicate further downside in price, but on the second test down the lows hold and the market reverses back up, showing large bars to the upside, which is a definite shift in momentum. Because of this shift in momentum, the trader attempting to short as price approaches the .618 retracement level would either stand aside and wait for further confirmation, use a very closely managed stop, or look for an entry to trade long, which may be found on a smaller time frame.

The market's job is to fool as many market participants as possible, and it is evident from this example that it did just that. This pattern formed prior to the Dow Jones Industrial Average reaching all-time highs above 12,000. When the market does fool many participants, it catches traders and investors off guard. Those who shorted believed that the price would continue lower based on the long, wide range bars. They were forced into covering or holding and painfully watching losses grow larger. This will create upside fuel for this pattern.

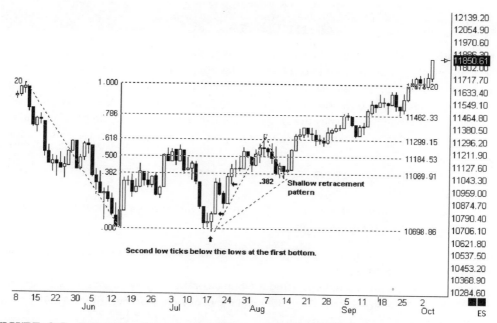

FIGURE 9.2 Daily view of the Double Bottom pattern on the Dow index. On this chart you can see that the price on the second bottom just barely ticks through the lows below reversing.

Also notice in Figure 9.1 the number of bars that formed after the first bottom formed. The retracement up was approximately three bars up, and then the second leg of the double bottom was approximately three bars down. When the time ratios are equal in length, as in this example, the pattern is generally more significant. This concept was first described by W.D. Gann in the 1920s, and he referred to it as the equal time phenomenon. This is another way of describing symmetry.

Looking for Trend Clues

Figure 9.2 offers a closer look at what is happening with the Dow index price than is clearly visible on the weekly chart in Figure 9.1. We will examine some clues in Figure 9.2 that the astute trader could use to determine a potential early trend reversal. We can see that the second low just barely ticked through the first low of the Double Bottom pattern before reversing. After the second low is made, long, wide range bars start to form to the upside. These are marked with arrows in Figure 9.2. The first retracement pattern that forms is able to retrace only to the .382 level. This, along with the wide range bars up, is an indication of a trend. We will cover ways to identify trends in Chapter 10 on trend identification of the S&P 500 market.

MANAGING COUNTERTREND TRADES IN A TREND ENVIRONMENT

At times traders will find themselves in a trade that is counter to the trend. It is imperative that upon realizing this or suspecting that a trend is developing against them, traders use trade management to control the risk in the trade and protect any profits. In Figure 9.3 we can see that the price does indeed turn down from the .618 level and has a move large enough to offer the trader profits. The price reaches the .382 retracement, and profits should be taken and the stop-loss order moved to breakeven. This accomplishes two very important tenets in trading:

1. Locking in a profit—always remember you are trading to make money, and not to prove that you are right.
2. Moving the stop down to breakeven after taking a partial profit reduces the risk in the trade and protects profits and capital.

This trade management can be applied to any of the patterns that are reversal patterns and the trader is in a countertrend trade.

Figure 9.4 shows an example of using a Fibonacci ratio to move a stop-loss order. The assumption is if the price exceeds the .786 it will move beyond that level to the 1.00 or to an extension ratio such as the 1.272 or 1.618.

FIGURE 9.3 Dow index daily chart example of a countertrend trade and managing risk and locking in a profit in a Double Bottom pattern.

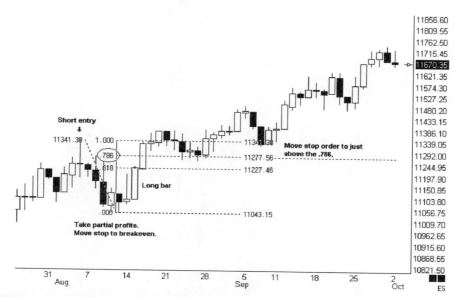

FIGURE 9.4 Dow index daily chart of Double Bottom pattern: managing countertrend trade using Fibonacci ratios to move stops and protect profits. The stop-loss order can be moved to just above the .786. The assumption is if the price exceeds the .786 level, it will move higher.

Double Top Pattern Example

Figure 9.5 shows an example of a Double Top pattern in the crude oil market that leads to a large decline. The second top does not exactly match the first top in price, but there is only a few cents' difference. Once the market turns down from the second top, it accelerates to the downside, as is visible with the gaps down and the long, wide range bars. A trader recognizing these warning signs would want to look for areas to trade with that trend and momentum. A smaller time frame could be used for entries.

Pattern Recognition

The Double Top and Bottom patterns should be easy to see and aesthetically pleasing to the eye. The key to these patterns is the formation of the second leg of the top or bottom. It is not unusual for the second low on a Double Bottom pattern to be exceeded by a small amount or the second high on a Double Top pattern to be exceeded by a small amount. The reason for this is that stops are placed just at or slightly beyond these levels and are taken out just as the market reverses. Refer back to Figure 9.2 for an example of the price exceeding the second low. The same principles for controlling risk and managing trades apply to both the Double Top pattern and the Double Bottom pattern.

FIGURE 9.5 Crude oil daily chart example of a Double Top pattern. The two highs are within 20 cents.

Failure Point

The technician should always be aware of where the failure points are on any technical pattern. This knowledge will help the trader to control risk and manage the trade by placing stops at the appropriate price levels. The failure point of the Double Top pattern would be at the high of the pattern. (Refer back to Figure 9.5.) If the price reversed back up to those highs, the trader would want to cover any short positions and look for a place to go long. The trader could use a buy-stop order just above the highs to let the market pull them into the trade. A stop-loss order could be placed based on a visible chart point or dollar amount.

The failure point on the Double Bottom pattern would be if price reversed back down through the lows. The trader could use a buy-stop order to let the market pull them into the trade and then place a stop-loss order based on a visual chart point or dollar amount. (Refer back to Figure 9.1.)

HEAD AND SHOULDERS PATTERN

The Head and Shoulders pattern is more complex in its structure than the Double Top and Bottom patterns. There are more swings involved with this pattern, and it is sometimes not identified until close to completion.

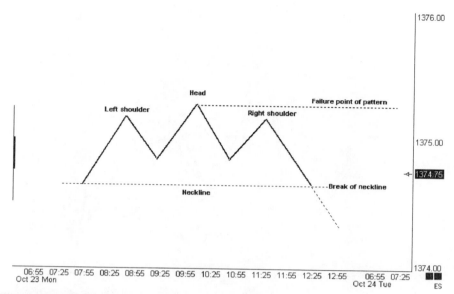

FIGURE 9.6 Head and Shoulders pattern—basic formation.

A combination of many of the patterns we have already covered in previous chapters of this book—AB=CD, Gartley, Butterfly, Three Drives, and other extension patterns—may be present in the formation of the Head and Shoulders pattern. Schabacker indicated this pattern was one of the seven cardinal patterns, which referred to common chart formations that had forecasting value that were accumulation or distribution reversal patterns.

The pattern is called Head and Shoulders because when viewing the pattern on a price chart the structure appears to form two shoulders and a head. See Figure 9.6 for an illustration of the Head and Shoulders pattern.

Applying Fibonacci Ratios to the Head and Shoulders Top Pattern

Let's take a look at a Head and Shoulders Top pattern that has Fibonacci ratios applied and has several other patterns as part of the structure. Figure 9.7 is a daily chart of IBM with a completed Head and Shoulders Top pattern. In this example you can see that the left shoulder also contains a Butterfly pattern and an AB=CD pattern. In the circled area you can see a Double Top pattern. In this case we have several patterns coming into the same price area as a potential top and reversal area.

The retracement in the left shoulder from point X to A to B came to above the .786 level. This is important to note, because how the right shoulder forms in relation to this

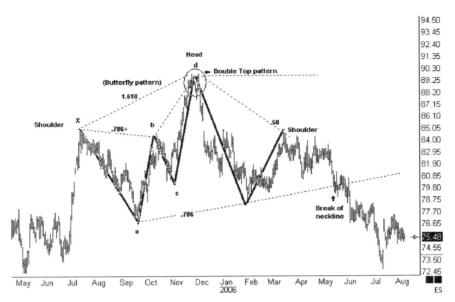

FIGURE 9.7 Daily chart of IBM with a Head and Shoulders Top pattern with Fibonacci ratios applied.

will give information as to the validity of this pattern and its potential strength or weakness, since the right shoulder is the reaction pattern coming after the high or head has been made. This countertrend rally will usually stop at the .618 or .786 level. When the right shoulder has a lower ratio than the left shoulder, it usually signifies a much more bearish pattern. Time symmetry is also important and places an added significance on the pattern if it is present.

Trading the Head and Shoulders Top Pattern

There several ways to approach trading this pattern, the first being that the trader is already short the market based on an extension pattern, such as the Butterfly and AB=CD pattern that can be seen in Figure 9.7, or possibly from the Double Top pattern that formed. This pattern is very easy to see after the full formation, but, as we indicated earlier, it is a little more difficult to spot sooner, before at least the top or head is complete and the first reaction down from there has taken place.

We will assume that if the trader is already positioned short in the market based on other patterns near the highs and has taken partial profits, the trader can then begin to look for signs of a right shoulder forming by a reaction rally back up, as outlined earlier. A stop-loss order could be kept at breakeven or just at the previous highs of the head,

FIGURE 9.8 IBM daily chart example of Head and Shoulders Top pattern showing stops moved as the price reaches the neckline level. The 1.272 extension of AD can be used for a profit objective.

because the pattern would be void if the price then exceeded this level. As mentioned previously, the majority of traders watch for a break of the neckline to enter the trade. Because of this, the trader positioned in this trade earlier would want to monitor the price for a break of the neckline for potential further gains.

There is always the possibility of any pattern failing, so the trader could also take a second profit as the neckline is being tested or broken and move the stop to just above the last high. Figure 9.8 shows an example of placing the stops and where the break of the neckline is. From that point, if prices continue further, the trader can then use either a 1.272 extension from the AD of the AB=CD pattern for further profits and trail a stop or a Fibonacci retracement from a larger swing.

Another traditional way to measure a profit objective with this pattern is to take the height of the pattern and project it down from the price level of the broken neckline. Figure 9.9 shows this example.

This pattern can also be entered using the break of the neckline by using a sell-stop order and letting the market pull you into the trade. A stop-loss order can be placed using a visual chart point or dollar amount.

Failure Point The failure point in this pattern is just above the formation of the head. Refer back to Figure 9.6. At this point the trader would look to go long by using a buy-stop

FIGURE 9.9 IBM daily chart example of Head and Shoulders Top pattern. The pattern height can be measured and projected down from the break of the neckline and used for a profit objective.

order. The stop-loss order can be placed using a visual chart point or dollar amount. Failure points and failed patterns will usually have a strong move in the opposite direction of the original pattern.

Head and Shoulders Bottom Pattern

Since we mentioned earlier that these patterns have been present in markets for centuries and have not changed, we will take this opportunity to show you an example of this repetition. Figure 9.10 is a Head and Shoulders Bottom pattern from 1928. It is an example from R.W. Schabacker's 1930 book, *Stock Market Theory and Practice*.

The chart is of Westinghouse Electric from 1928 (i.e., prior to the crash of 1929). In this figure, A, B, and C are used to label the left shoulder, head, and right shoulder of the pattern (the Bottom pattern is an inverted Head and Shoulders Top pattern). If we were to remove the labeling of this chart and the year it is from, it would be indistinguishable from any price chart today that forms the same pattern.

On the left-hand side of Figure 9.10 you can see an AB=CD pattern that forms and is completed at the point labeled A, or the bottom of the left shoulder. A small sell AB=CD then forms following the completion of the left shoulder and makes a new low to complete the point of the head.

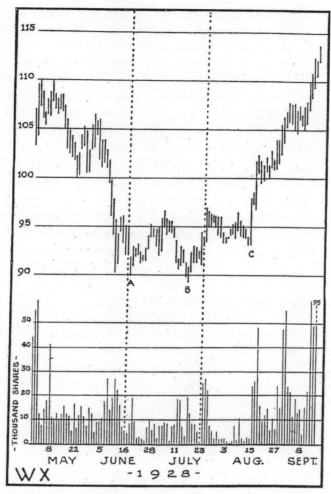

FIGURE 9.10 Head and Shoulders Bottom pattern from *Stock Market Theory and Practice*.
Source: R.W. Schabacker, *Stock Market Theory and Practice* (B.C. Forbes, 1930).

Once the price moves up from the point labeled B or the bottom of the head, you can see long bars where the neckline is broken, and then a small buy AB=CD before the price accelerates to the upside. The price does not quite make it down to the .618 retracement of BC, the completion of the head and the completion of the right shoulder, which, as we discussed earlier, would have been a sign of strength. Again, this is a sign of a shift of momentum to the upside. The same trading techniques and risk management apply to this chart from 1928 as to any other chart in this book.

The caption at the bottom of the page states that it is an irregular Head and Shoulders Bottom pattern. Schabacker says of this chart that no chart picked at random from actual market history will ever show a perfect formation. He does not consider this pattern perfect because the head of the pattern, B, does not go as low as it could have, and the right shoulder does not retrace as deeply as it could have to form a perfect Head and Shoulders pattern. We thought it both interesting and educational to show this particular example that illustrates these imperfections. It is not often that we get perfect patterns. The longer a trader studies any pattern, the easier it is to identify the acceptable imperfect patterns and distinguish them from ones that are invalid.

Failure Point   By now you probably know the failure point of this pattern. It is below B, the completion of the head. If the price were to reverse and make new lows below that point, the pattern would be considered a failed pattern. Once the momentum shifts up and starts making higher lows and higher highs, an astute trader could even use the point below C, the completion of the right shoulder, for a failure point.

BROADENING TOP AND BOTTOM PATTERNS

Schabacker credits A.W. Wetzel with first publicly identifying the Broadening Top and Bottom patterns. In his book *Stock Market Theory and Practice*, Schabacker refers to this pattern as one of the seven formations that indicate preparation for a major movement. This pattern was seen in many stocks in the third quarter of 1929 preceding the crash of October and the bear market that followed.

This pattern is rare, and Schabacker stated that because of this it was less important as an indicator than the more common reversal patterns. This does not in any way mean that it is not a powerful pattern when it does form.

This pattern was marketed by J. Welles Wilder 50 or so years later as the Reverse Point Wave system. It was sold at the time for about $2,500 to almost 1,000 traders. It is also covered in H.M. Gartley's 1935 book, *Profits in the Stock Market*, where it is referred to as the T-6 Broadening Top.

Pattern Structure

The structure of this pattern consists of five reversal points. Each low is successively lower and each high successively higher. Figure 9.11 shows a Broadening Top formation in the Dow Jones Industrial Average preceding the price highs of 2000 and the bear market that ensued.

The Broadening Top and Bottom patterns are really nothing more than triangle and coil patterns, which are classic technical analysis patterns in which the market comes

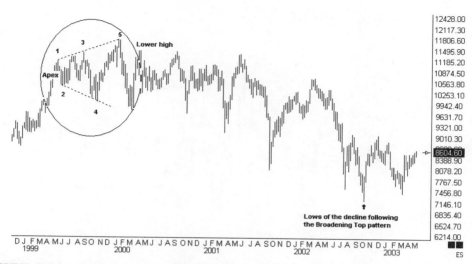

FIGURE 9.11 Dow Jones Industrial Average weekly chart of a Broadening Top pattern shows five reversal points and the apex on the left side. Many stocks in the third quarter of 1929 formed this pattern preceding the October crash.

to a point of indecision before breaking out to either the upside or downside. They can also be continuation type patterns found in trends. Refer to Chapter 10, "Learning to Recognize Trend Days." The apex of the pattern is reversed from a traditional and more commonly found triangle pattern. The apex is on the left side of the pattern rather than on the right side and expands from there. The pattern is sometimes referred to as an Expanding Triangle pattern.

You can see in Figure 9.11 that following the decline after point 5 there is a rally that would be considered a sixth reversal point, but the rally does not exceed point 5. The establishment of this lower high indicates the probability of a reversal.

Adding Fibonacci Ratios

We can define the waves in most Broadening Top and Bottom patterns by the use of Fibonacci numbers. Each wave in the pattern is interrelated by these numbers. The most common Fibonacci numbers that will be seen and used in this pattern are .618, .786, 1.00, 1.272, and 1.618.

Figure 9.12 shows a portion of the Dow index chart used in Figure 9.11 with the addition of Fibonacci ratios to define the geometric structure.

The left side of the pattern from points 1 through 3 forms a 1.272 extension pattern. You can also see the formation of a Three Drives pattern, which completes at point 3 of

FIGURE 9.12 Dow index weekly chart of Broadening Top pattern with Fibonacci ratios added to define the geometric structure.

the Broadening Top pattern. There is also a small AB=CD that completes at the top of the pattern. Point 3 is higher than point 1.

Points 2 through 4 form another 1.272 extension pattern. This pattern extends just a bit beyond the 1.272. Point 4 is lower than point 2. One last 1.272 extension pattern forms from point 4 to point 5 to complete the pattern. A note here on the final wave completion at point 5: An extension up to the 2.00 is acceptable, but anything beyond that signals the market is in a strongly trending mode.

The lower high that would be the sixth point rally completes at the .786 retracement of the initial decline from point 5. In this example the pattern is very symmetrical and the waves are easily identifiable.

The formation of a Broadening Bottom pattern is just the opposite of the Broadening Top pattern. (See Figure 9.13 for an example of a Broadening Bottom pattern.) You can see in this example that the corn market takes off and goes into a very strong uptrend after completing the pattern.

The low points 1, 3, and 5 do not reach the 1.272 extension—they just exceed the 1.00. Symmetrically this pattern is almost perfect. The time it takes to form the lows between points 1 and 3 and again between 3 and 5 is almost identical, as is illustrated in Figure 9.13.

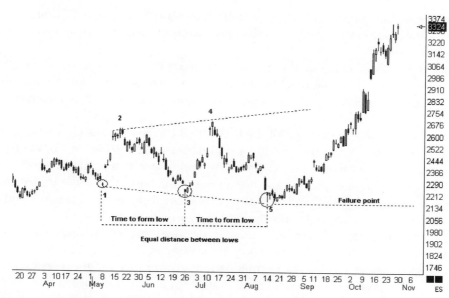

FIGURE 9.13 Corn daily chart example of Broadening Bottom pattern. Although the lows do not quite reach the 1.272 extensions, the times between lows are almost identical.

Failure Point

Both Figures 9.12 and 9.13 have the failure points of the Broadening Top and Bottom patterns marked. These patterns are seen at tops and bottoms on longer-term time frames; they can form on smaller time frames, but when found on the longer-term time frames they can signal a major reversal. This is evident in the example of the Broadening Top pattern of the Dow index (refer back to Figure 9.12).

When these patterns fail, they can lead to explosive moves in the opposite direction (i.e., continuing in the direction of the original trend). When point 5, which should be the completion point of the pattern, explodes with a wide range bar (usually two to three times the length of an average daily bar) or a price gap occurs, a continuation move of major proportions is most likely under way. As always, the trader must quantify the risk and use stop-loss protection when trading this pattern.

Trading the Broadening Top and Bottom Patterns

As is noted and depicted in the example charts of this pattern, it is not unusual to see other patterns form as a Broadening Top or Bottom pattern is forming. In Figure 9.12 we can see an AB=CD pattern, a 1.272 extension pattern, and a Three Drives pattern. When entering a trade into a Broadening Top or Bottom pattern, the trader can use any of these other patterns as entries and any of the stop-loss and profit objective techniques we have already discussed.

Using the example in Figure 9.12 of the Broadening Top pattern, a retracement entry could be used after the initial reaction down and a stop-loss order placed above either the .786 or the 1.00 if the risk is acceptable. A trailing stop can be used for managing exits on the trade.

In the case of the Broadening Bottom in Figure 9.13, the example shows there is not much of a retracement; the trader who is waiting for a 1.272 to enter would miss the initial entry. The trader would probably want to scale down to a smaller time frame for a pattern to enter on and place a stop-loss order. If the pattern is being traded from a longer-term time frame such as a daily or weekly chart, keep in mind that it could be a longer-term reversal signal and you may want to plan exits accordingly.

If either pattern has a failure and turns up or down through the failure points, the trader would want to then look for an entry in the direction of that failure.

Although a Broadening Top or Bottom pattern is rarer than others presented in this book, it can be one of the most reliable and profitable patterns and is certainly worth the trader's time to study.

CHAPTER 10

Learning to Recognize Trend Days

A trend day can easily become a countertrend trader's largest loss day as a result of repeatedly trying to trade against the trend. A trend day can be defined as a market where price opens on or near its highs or lows and then closes at the opposite end of the range. These traders may feel they are doing the right thing by taking the countertrend signals or patterns but repeatedly get stopped out. A day like that can erase weeks or even months of profits. Not only can it damage the trader financially, but it can also damage the trader's mind-set. Conversely, if a trader learns to identify trend days and trade in the direction of the trend, the trader can turn that around and trend days can be their best trading days.

In this chapter we want to present examples of trend days that occur in the S&P 500 E-mini market. We chose this market for a couple of reasons; first, it is a widely traded market by day traders, and second, the characteristics illustrated in this market can also be used with individual stocks or other markets. Since the S&P 500 index has a total of 500 stocks, it would stand to reason that if the index is trending, a large majority of the stocks in that index will also be trending. The main purpose of including this chapter is to help countertrend traders become aware of when a trend is present so that they can make well-informed trading decisions that will help them to protect capital and learn to trade in the direction of the short-term trend in this market.

The areas we cover are:

- Identifying a trend day.
- Patterns found on trend days.
- Combining time frames and using Fibonacci ratios on trend days.

- Avoiding countertrend trades on a trend day and controlling risk on a trend day.
- Example of trading a trend day.

IDENTIFYING A TREND DAY

We first define a trend as higher highs and higher lows in an uptrend and lower highs and lower lows in a downtrend. (See Figures 10.1 and 10.2.) Trends can manifest on any time frame, short or long, and for trends longer in duration the trend will be seen first on the shorter time frames. Strong trends will open or close on or near the lows or highs and close at the opposite end of the range. It is a mistake to assume when a trend is in progress that a price has gone too high so therefore it is a short sale or it has gone too low and therefore it is a buy. Prices can always move further up or down than anyone expects. The percentage of trend days is much smaller than the percentage of range or countertrend type days. A typical trading month may see anywhere from two to five trend days on average.

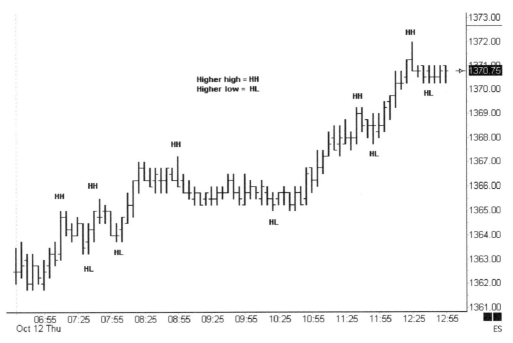

FIGURE 10.1 Example of a short-term 5-minute chart uptrend in the S&P 500 E-mini market. Higher highs and higher lows define the uptrend. On this day the market opens near the lows and closes near the highs.

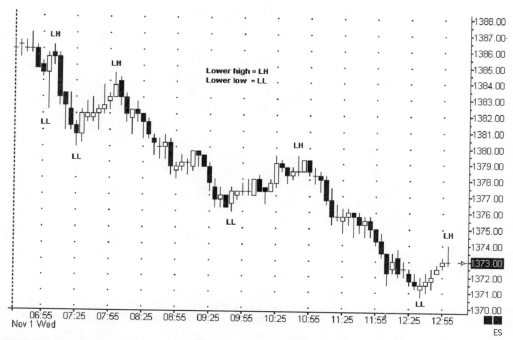

FIGURE 10.2 Example of a short-term 5-minute chart downtrend in the S&P 500 E-mini market. Lower highs and lower lows define the downtrend. Just the opposite of Figure 10.1, the market opens near the highs and closes near the lows.

When trading from a short time frame such as a 5-minute chart, the trader should be aware that a trend can manifest at any point during the trading day and end at any point in the trading day. In other words, sometimes trends can be short-lived.

Figure 10.3 is a price chart of the same time period as Figure 10.1. Figure 10.3 shows a more condensed view that gives us a little more data to work with. In this example we can see the market gapping up on the open. This tells us there is an imbalance of price. The vertical grid line marks the opening price on the day, and to the left is the previous day's closing price bar. The important point to note here is how the market holds the gap open. In Figure 10.3 we can see how the market holds the gap with no attempt to retrace back into the gap and fill in the price void. This is our first sign of strength and an indication that an uptrend may be in the making for the day. We can also see marked in Figure 10.3 a long, wide range bar that makes new highs on the day; this also can be an early indication of a trend day. If the price had reversed back into the gap after making the long, wide range bar with new highs, then a trend day would have most likely not been in progress.

FIGURE 10.3 Example of a short-term 5-minute chart uptrend in the S&P 500 E-mini market. The price holds the gap-up open and makes no attempt to fill the gap. A long, wide range bar makes highs on the day, a sign of strength and an indication that an uptrend may be in progress.

The markets are constantly in a process of either contracting (i.e., trading in a range), which gives us the countertrend trading setups, or expanding, which gives us trends. There are three market tendencies that can alert the trader to the possibility of a trend day developing.

1. A narrowing of range, referred to as an NR7, which is defined as the narrowest range in the past seven trading days. This was first published by Toby Crabel in *Day Trading with Short Term Price Patterns and Opening Range Breakout* (Traders Press, 1990). Linda Raschke also has done extensive research using narrow range trading days as a characteristic that can precede a trend day.
2. Gap opening followed by long, wide range bars in the first 15 to 30 minutes of trading.
3. Neutral market closes, where the market closes in the same area that it opened.

Both Toby Crabel and Linda Raschke have done excellent statistical research on these market tendencies that precede trends.

When a trend day does develop, it will be most valid when all indexes—S&P 500, Dow Jones Industrial Average, NASDAQ, and Russell—are trending in the same direction. In an uptrend they would each be making new highs; they would make new lows in a downtrend. As mentioned earlier, the majority of stocks that make up these indexes will be trending in the same direction. If traders see individual stocks that are not participating in the trend, they should make a note of those and watch for patterns to develop to trade those stocks. And if they see stocks that are leading the trend, they can also make a note of those stocks to watch for setups in the direction of the trend.

PATTERNS FOUND ON TREND DAYS

Once traders have identified that a trend is under way, they will do best trading in the direction of the trend. There are specific patterns that tend to form during these trends. As we have mentioned previously, any retracements that are pullbacks in a trend will most likely reach only the .382 for the strongest trends, and the .50 for other trends. There may or may not be an AB=CD pattern with these retracements, and the trader may want to watch for consolidation-type patterns to form and use repetitive correction sizes to time entries into trades. Most of the corrections or pullbacks that occur during a trend day will be shallow. The strongest trends will tend to correct between 1.25 and 3.5 points. Generally, any corrections or pullbacks in a trend will not exceed 5.5 points. The exception to this is in a high volatility environment where corrections may exceed 5.5 points. The corrections may be 8–15 points or higher depending on the volatility. This helps the trader to place stops when trading a trend day.

We will focus on these two trend day patterns:

1. AB=CD correction
2. Consolidation pattern

AB=CD Pattern on a Trend Day

Most intraday trends will see at least one small AB=CD pattern form that will give the trader a low-risk entry into the trend. As mentioned earlier, the corrections tend to be shallow, and many times the small AB=CD patterns that form will retrace to the .382 or to the .50. On a true trend day they will usually not retrace to the .618 or the .786 once the trend is under way. In Figure 10.4, two AB=CD patterns form during the trading day on a 5-minute chart. The first AB=CD pattern forms early in the day and before the trend is in full progress. This first pattern does retrace to the .618. Notice the size of the correction: 4.5 points. The corrections tend to be very similar in size on a trend day. On very strong trend days and if the trend accelerates, the corrections will become shallower. Trends are one of the few times we use the .382 or .50 retracement as an entry into a trade.

The second AB=CD pattern that forms later in the trading day is one point less than the first AB=CD correction at 3.5 points. Notice in Figure 10.5 that the retracement uses

FIGURE 10.4 5-minute chart showing two AB=CD corrections in trend day down. The first AB=CD correction pattern forms shortly after the opening and retraces to the .618.

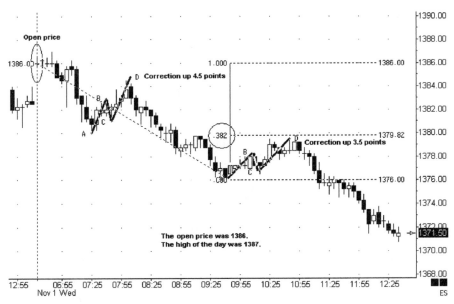

FIGURE 10.5 5-minute chart showing two AB=CD corrections in trend day down. Using the opening price rather than the high, the AB=CD pattern completes at the .382 level.

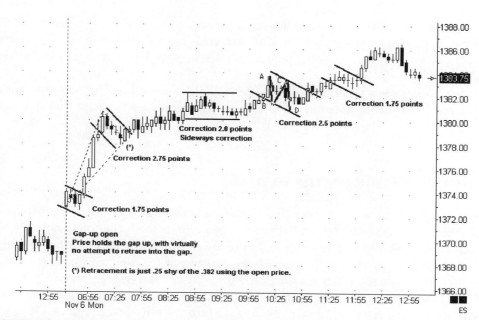

FIGURE 10.6 5-minute chart of trend day up. The market gaps up on the open, and the price does not fill the gap. The corrections are shallow and repetitive.

the open price at 1386 rather than the actual high of the swing. On trend days the price tends to retrace to the .382 level from the open price. There will usually be one AB=CD pattern that retraces to the .382 using the open price. It is good to be aware of this, as it may help the trader time an entry into a trade.

Trend Day Consolidation Pattern

Although the AB=CD pattern is a consolidation pattern on a trend day, consolidation patterns can also form that are absent of an AB=CD. These patterns may form as bull flags in an uptrend and bear flags in a downtrend. Triangle patterns may also form as a consolidation pattern along with sideways-type consolidation in very strong trends.

In Figure 10.6 the trend day starts with a gap-up open. The price does not attempt to fill in the gap area and instead makes a very shallow retracement of only 1.75 points before making highs on the day. The bars making highs that lead to the next correction of only 2.75 points are long bars, which shows strength in the market. The retracement from the second correction of 2.75 points is just shy of the .382 using the open price.

Notice the third correction up of only 2.0 points; this correction is very shallow as price consolidates and is considered a sideways correction. Once again the market is showing us there is strength behind this move up and the trend is likely to continue into the close. If you look closely at the fourth correction on the chart, you can see a small AB=CD correction that is only 2.5 points, another very shallow correction in a strong trend up.

Once traders see a repetition of corrections in the same range, they can use that to time an entry into a consolidation pattern. These tendencies are the same for trend days down.

FIBONACCI RATIOS ON TREND DAYS

Generally, when a trend on a short time frame such as a 5-minute chart is progressing throughout the trading day, the trader wants to be aware of the higher time frame cycles. The markets are usually traveling to a higher or lower level based on a larger time frame. Look at Figure 10.7 and notice how this 60-minute chart with seven bars enclosed within the dotted rectangle shows us a view of the price from the trend day shown in Figure 10.6. We can clearly see how strong the momentum is looking at this 60-minute chart. We can see the gap-up open, and we can also see how the price reacted at the Fibonacci retracement levels.

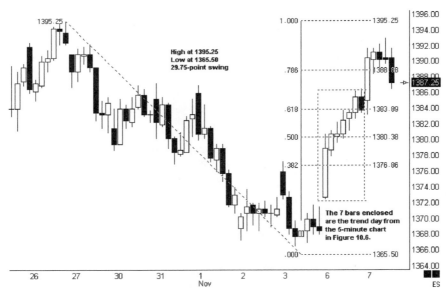

FIGURE 10.7 60-minute chart showing the larger cycle at work: the trend day from Figure 10.6 enclosed in the dotted rectangle.

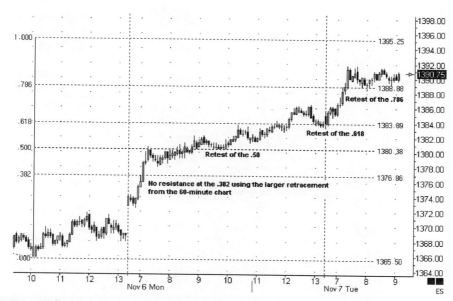

FIGURE 10.8 5-minute chart showing the 60-minute 29.75 swing and the Fibonacci retracement levels. Using the retracement levels from the 60-minute chart applied to a 5-minute chart, we can get a close-up view of how the price reacts at the resistance levels.

At the first .382 retracement in Figure 10.7, there is a long, wide range bar that easily slices through this level with no resistance. Refer now to Figure 10.8, which shows an interesting close-up view of price action using the retracement from the 60-minute time frame applied to the 5-minute chart. We can see that when the price reaches the .382 shortly after the gap-up open, it slices right through the .382 price level with no resistance. This move is the first long bar seen on the 60-minute chart in Figure 10.7, and in Figure 10.8 we are looking at the same long bar broken down into a 5-minute time frame. The price then goes up to the .50 level and finds very little resistance there as well.

This information is very valuable because it tells us that the price is in a trend and is likely to get to at least the larger .618 or the .786 and possibly higher using the 60-minute time frame. It is also important because it tells the countertrend trader to avoid countertrend trades and to trade with the trend. We can also see in Figure 10.8 how, once the price is around the Fibonacci retracement levels from the 60-minute time frame and applied to the 5-minute time frame, the consolidations are a test and retest of the levels once they are broken.

The next thing we want to look at is where the consolidation patterns that are outlined in Figure 10.6 are consolidating. Figure 10.9 shows us these same consolidation patterns but puts them into perspective with the 60-minute Fibonacci retracement

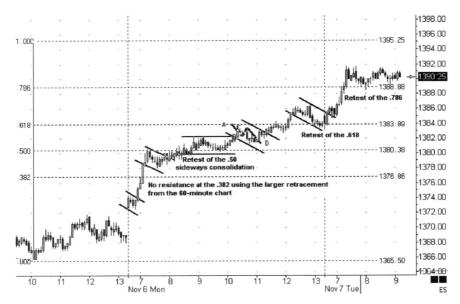

FIGURE 10.9 5-minute chart with 60-minute Fibonacci retracement levels applied, showing consolidation patterns that formed at Fibonacci levels during the trend day.

levels. We can see that the price reacts in a trendlike manner at the Fibonacci resistance levels. At each level the price forms a consolidation pattern before moving higher.

If we look at the .50, .618, and .786 levels, we can see that the price consolidated above each of these levels; this is usually an indication that the price is in a trend and is going to move higher. The .50 level shows the sideways consolidation pointed out earlier in Figure 10.6 and how bullish the price is with only a 2.0-point pullback above the resistance area. This is why it is so important for the trader to learn to identify a trend and to take appropriate trading actions. It would have been a disastrous day for a countertrend trader to have attempted selling into this strength.

CONTROLLING RISK ON A TREND DAY

If countertrend traders inadvertently find themselves in a trend day, they can make a graceful exit by using the consolidation patterns as an exit. Referring back to Figure 10.9 as an example, let's assume a trader sells the market at the .618 retracement level and initiates a 3-point stop, only realizing that a trend day is in progress once in the trade. At this point, to control the risk and protect capital, the trader wants to utilize one or more of these trade management techniques:

- Ensure a stop-loss order is in place to prevent a small loss from turning into a large loss.
- Use the small pullbacks to exit if possible.
- Put the stop-loss order just above or below the last small swing high or low.

Again, refer to Figure 10.9 and the .618 level, and let's assume the trader is short from the 1383.75 level with a three-point stop and the initial objective was another .618 retracement down. The trader would have an opportunity to exit at least part of position as the small AB=CD pattern forms and to pull the stop down to breakeven. This would allow a small profit even in a countertrend trade. If the trader either does not exit or enters the trade at the second test up of the .618 and then realizes he is caught in a trend, he can either:

- Exit the trade immediately and reverse.
- Use the next small pullback to exit, realizing it may be very shallow.
- Pull the stop down to the last small high.

Again, in either case a stop-loss order must be in the market to control losses. When traders see prices consolidating on top of Fibonacci levels in an uptrend or below in a downtrend, they must realize that the probability is in favor of the price continuing in the direction of the trend.

TRADING A TREND DAY

We now look at a few examples of entering trades from our chart examples, placing stop-loss orders and profit objectives. We use the same trend day charts we have been viewing for our first trade example. We also look at a failed trend day trade example, because, as we have mentioned, nothing in trading is ever 100 percent.

Trade Setup: Trend Day Up

Market: S&P E-mini

Contracts: 2

Ideally, on a trend day the trader would want to hold a core position that is initiated early in the day and try to hold the position into the close. The assumption is that a true trend day will open on or near its lows and close on or near its lows. The trader can then take off contracts and add them back on as the trend day patterns form. This will lock

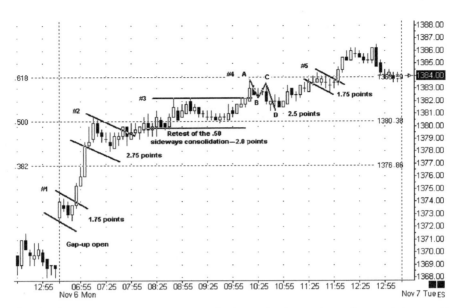

FIGURE 10.10 Five trend day patterns marked on a 5-minute chart of a trend day up. Note the size of the corrections; the market will tend to repeat the correction size.

in profits and reduce risk in the event that the trend ends prematurely before the close of the market, and it will keep the trader in the market for the bulk of the trend.

In Figure 10.10 there are five trend day patterns marked in the chart, and we will review those:

1. Consolidation pattern shortly after gap-up open of 1.75 points.

2. Consolidation pattern at the .50 resistance area of 2.75 points.

3. Sideways consolidation pattern above the .50 retracement level. The correction is 2.0 points.

4. Small AB=CD pattern with a 2.5-point correction.

5. Small consolidation pattern of 1.75 points at the .618 level.

Using pattern #1, if the trader has enough market knowledge and skill to identify an early trend condition off the open, he would have a very early start into this trend day. Instead, we assume that the trend is identified only after pattern #1 because of the conditions mentioned earlier:

- Gap-up open not filled by price.
- Long, wide range bars.
- Shallow first correction.

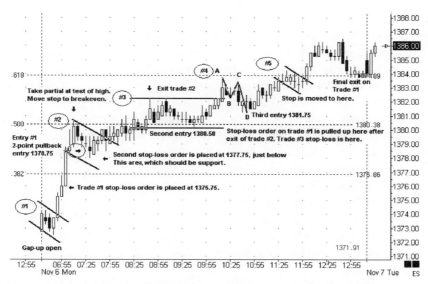

FIGURE 10.11   5-minute chart of trend day up, showing entry into a consolidation pattern using a 3-point stop-loss placed just below the long, wide range bar, which should act as support.

The trader waits for the first trend entry pattern to form, which is at pattern #2. We know the first pullback is only 1.75 points, and we want to use an entry between this and a 3-point pullback to enter. If we use a 2- to 3-point correction and a 3-point initial stop, that will give the market room to wiggle around a little and allow the trader to place the stop-loss order just around the 5.5-point trend pullback level that we do not want to see the market violate in order for the trend to be valid. There are always going to be exceptions to every rule, but we have found this to be a good general rule for trend days.

If we use 2 points from the high of pattern #2, this gives us an entry of 1378.75. Using an initial stop-loss order of 3 points, that will place the stop at 1375.75, which is just below the low of the long, wide range bar that should act as support, as seen in Figure 10.11. This gives us an acceptable stop-loss placement.

The first profit objective is going to be a test of the last highs at 1378.50. Once this is filled, the trader wants to move the stop-loss order up to breakeven to lock in a profit and reduce risk in the trade. Remember that the trader wants to try to hold a partial position into the close on a trend day, so the next step is to wait for the next pattern and then add on one more contract. The number of contracts is totally dependent on the money management plan of the trader. We are using an example of two contracts to illustrate how the trade can be managed on a trend day. In this example the trader has a 2-point profit with the stop at breakeven.

The next entry forms at pattern #3 with the sideways consolidation above the .50. When the trader sees price consolidating above a Fibonacci resistance level (or below on a trend day down), this is a sign of strength, and the trader may use that as a low-risk entry. The premise is simple: What was once resistance is now support. The opposite would be true in a downtrend: What was once support is now resistance.

We can use that information to our advantage and enter the second trade in the trend day. We can place an order to go long just above the .50 at 1380.50 and place a stop one tick below the last consolidation level at 1377.75 for a 2.75 stop. The stop on the first position can be maintained at 1378.75. The profit target again is at a retest of the last high at 1382.25. This would gain 1.75 points, and the stop on the first position can be moved to 1380.00, just below the last low. This leaves one open position that the trader is trying to press for further gains on the trend day.

The third entry comes at the completion of the small AB=CD of pattern #4. Again, be aware of the pullback sizes that have already occurred. We can determine that the pattern completes around 1381.75, which is a 2-point pullback from the last high. We can place the stop-loss order just below the last low, along with the other stop-loss order on the core at 1380.00. The exit is at the retest of the last high at 1383.75 for a gain of 2 points on that contract.

Pattern #5 is the last consolidation pattern shown on this chart, and the pullback is only 2 points. This most likely would be a tough entry because of the shallow pullback, and in real-life trading sometimes you just miss it. The trader, however, would still have the initial core trade on from 1378.75 and the stop-loss order on that position at 1380.00. Once pattern #5 makes new highs, the stop-loss order on the 1378.75 position can be moved up to one tick below the low of that pattern at 1382.50. The trader would then want to look for a spot to exit at or near the close. The closing price is 1384, and that would yield 5.25 points on the initial core position. If the trader had been able to enter earlier off the open, the gains would, of course, be larger. Take some time to study Figure 10.11 and the trades presented with that chart.

Trade Setup: Failed Trend Day Up

Market: S&P E-mini

Contracts: 2

In the next chart example, Figure 10.12, we look at the importance of maintaining the stop-loss levels as the trade progresses and of always remembering that any type of pattern can fail. It will serve the trader in the long run to focus on preserving capital by keeping losses small and protecting profits.

We have already covered that any correction beyond a 5.5-point correction is likely to signal a trend change on the 5-minute chart. We can see in Figure 10.12 that the day starts

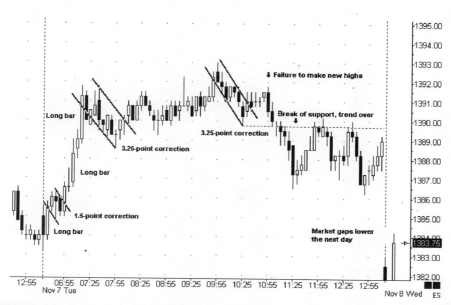

FIGURE 10.12 5-minute chart of failed trend day up. Once the market fails to make new highs and turns lower, the trend is over.

out in a trend day fashion; there are long bars and shallow corrections. The important items to note in this chart are:

- After the high and the second 3.25-point correction are made, the market then fails to make a new high.
- Remember that on a strong trend day the market will continue to make higher highs and higher lows on an uptrend day and lower highs and lower lows on a downtrend day.
- Once the market turns down and makes a new low that is marked break of support on the chart, that trend is most likely over.

A trader using good trade management techniques would give back very little profit. The market also gaps down lower on the next open. It is wise to listen to what the market is telling us.

If you are not familiar with trend days, take some time to observe and learn the characteristics and to become adept at trading them. We suggest keeping a file of charts of trends and making observational notes of the repetitive characteristics. Once you are comfortable with trend days, you can formulate a trading plan for them that utilizes proper money management, entry strategies, and stop-loss placement and profit objectives.

PART III

Essential Elements of Trading

CHAPTER 11

Trade Management

Learning to manage trades as efficiently as possible will have a large impact on the trader's bottom line over time. This skill usually requires much practice, time, and patience on the trader's part. It also requires traders to take an objective look at their trading, trade by trade, to recognize the areas that are going well and the areas that need work.

The first step in refining trading as a skill is to learn a method of trading that suits the trader's personality. Understanding trading from a perspective of probabilities, meaning that any good method of trading will have periods of profit and periods of loss, will point the trader in the right direction for developing and adhering to money management rules.

It is impossible to predict in what order wins and losses will occur. When a period of loss does happen, the trader must continue studying the method to learn how to trade through those periods. Unfortunately, it is at this point that the vast majority of traders learning the method will abandon it and search for a method that does not incur the inevitable drawdown. It is learning to manage the risk and losses during periods of drawdown that will eventually make a profound positive impact on the bottom line.

Money management combined with developing excellent trade management skills will eventually be the heart and soul of each successful trader. We have covered many trade management options as we presented each pattern. Take time to study and review these; we encourage you to adapt the trade management to your own trading style, time frame, and market that is suited to your personality.

In this chapter we present a straightforward approach to allocating capital to each trade, including figuring the position size for each trade. There are many good books on money management as it applies to trading, and again we encourage you to study this topic in depth so that you have a thorough understanding of its importance to your success in trading. One book in particular that stands out as a recommendation for traders of all levels is *Trading Risk: Enhanced Profitability through Risk Control* by Kenneth L. Grant.

We also cover the warning signs and confirmation signs that have been discussed in previous chapters. Learning these as an important part of the overall trading skills will help the trader manage trades properly by either staying on the sidelines when market conditions warrant, waiting for further confirmation to enter a trade, or pressing for additional profits.

Learning to think in probabilities—understanding that there is a random outcome to each individual trade and that over a period of time the trading method has a positive expectation—is a learning process in itself. We address that first so that the reader can begin to think about and understand this important concept.

THINKING IN PROBABILITIES

Money management is primarily a function of risk control. It is not possible to predict within a series of trades which ones will be winners and which ones will be losers. Another factor that cannot be predicted with 100 percent accuracy is the amount of profit that a trade will produce. That leaves one element of the trading equation that can be controlled—the risk factor. It is a natural thinking process of most traders to focus on how much money can be made on a trade. Unfortunately, one important aspect is often overlooked: how much can be lost. The trader must learn to focus on controlling the risk of loss in each trade. This can be accomplished by applying sound money management techniques, which include:

- Allocating small percentages of total trading capital to each trade.
- Using stop-loss protection.
- Taking profits when available.

It is important to understand that the trader must keep trading—continue pulling the handle, so to speak, as in playing a casino slot machine. We are not suggesting that any trader overtrade; rather, we are suggesting that when their edge is present they trade it each and every time.

We mention casino slot machines here because there is an important correlation, and that is in the edge. Casinos have an edge, and successful traders have an edge. Casinos know the percentage edge they maintain over the players and play each hand. If you have ever watched a blackjack dealer at a casino, you probably have never seen (and will never see) any dealer pass on a hand or deviate from the house rules. However, on the other side of the table you can observe blackjack players doing the opposite most of the time. Decisions are made based on emotions, and the higher the stakes, the higher the emotions. Usually when players base decisions on emotions they destroy any edge they may have had. The casino has a positive expectancy of winning over time, and the random gambler a negative expectation of winning over time.

How do traders learn to think in probabilities? It's a process that gaining market experience and skill will teach. Thinking in probabilities is first intellectualized by the trader. It is then brought into the trading process by the trader correctly executing a series of trades that begin to incorporate the concept into the experience of trading. It then becomes something the trader does without thinking; it becomes an inherent and essential part of the trading process and the trader.

In his book *Trading in the Zone*, Mark Douglas eloquently and thoroughly outlines and describes this process and gives excellent exercises to learn to think in probabilities. We have included this classic book in the recommended reading section in the back of this book.

Traders must set up their trading so that they are trading a plan in a repetitious manner so as to determine if there is an edge present. The plan must be traded over a large sample of trades to be able to analyze this. Once traders can tell statistically that there is an edge present, they can then begin to see that there are winning streaks and losing streaks present. They can then understand how valuable a well-thought-out trading plan with sound money management principles is.

One thing that is certain is that if the trader alters the edge of the trading method by taking random trades that are not part of the trading method, or late entries, early exits, and the like, it will be difficult to ever learn trading as being probabilistic. Take the approach to learn the good execution skills and trade management skills necessary to let the edge play out.

WARNING SIGNS AND CONFIRMATION SIGNS

As mentioned previously, the trader must learn to recognize varying market conditions that will either increase or decrease the probability of a successful trade. We do this by using specific warning signs and confirmation signs.

Warning Signs

These are the primary warning signs that we use to either prevent us from entering a trade or alert us to wait for signs that the momentum has slowed enough to enter the trade:

- Gaps in the CD leg.
- Long, wide range bars at or toward the completion point.

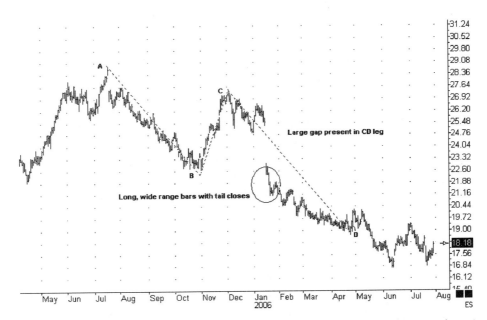

FIGURE 11.1 Intel (INTC) daily chart with warning signs present in the CD leg: gap down in the CD leg, long range bars, tail closes, and steep angle of the CD leg.

- Tail closes at or near the pattern completion point.
- Very steep CD leg as compared to the AB leg.

When monitoring an entry, the trader wants to look at the structure of the pattern and be alert for the aforementioned warning signs. Figure 11.1 shows an AB=CD pattern that formed on a daily chart of Intel (INTC). We can see a large gap present in the CD leg, long range bars, and tail closes. These warning signs are telling the trader there is excessive downward momentum in this stock, and the price could exceed the D completion point. The price move down caused by the large gap is a steep descent in the CD leg and is also a warning for the trader.

Confirmation Signs

Now we look at the daily INTC chart in Figure 11.2 and see how we could use confirmation techniques to enter the trade at a low-risk point. The primary confirmation signs we use are:

- Tweezer bottom or top.
- Gap in the direction of the trade.

FIGURE 11.2 Intel (INTC) daily chart showing confirmation signs for trade entry. Confirmation techniques allow a low-risk entry point into this trade.

- Tail closes or long, wide range bars in the direction of the trade.
- Confirmation bar—waiting one time bar before entering the trade.

Looking at Figure 11.2, on the left side of the chart we can see the original pattern completion point of D as was outlined in Figure 11.1. The pattern completion at point D is two full points above where the stock actually turned up. Had traders been patient and waited for a slowing of momentum using one of the aforementioned confirmation techniques, they would have been able to locate a low-risk entry point.

The tweezer bottoms and the gap-up open are certainly signs of slowing momentum to the downside and potential for the price to turn up. The risk in the trade could be easily quantified by placing a stop below the tweezer bottoms.

The technique of waiting one time bar on the time frame the trader is trading (i.e., daily time frame waits one daily bar, 5-minute time frame waits one 5-minute bar, etc.) can be implemented once the trader has seen tweezer bottoms, a gap in the direction of the trade, or long range bars in the direction of the trade. In the example shown in Figure 11.2, the daily bar on the day of the gap-up open would have been the entry bar for the trader following the tweezer bottom. This would have allowed the trader to place the stop-loss order just below the tweezer bottom and would have provided a low-risk entry point.

FIGURE 11.3 NASDAQ-100 (QQQQ) daily chart of AB=CD sell pattern with warning signs. Three gap-up openings and wide range bars are definite warning signs for this AB=CD pattern.

Waiting one time bar can be used when the trader has reason to believe, based on price behavior, that price may exceed the completion point of a pattern. This is never a guarantee of a profitable trade, but it does give the trader a tool to use in varying market conditions.

Let's take a look at an example of a chart that is showing definite warning signs up to the completion point. Figure 11.3 shows an AB=CD sell pattern. There are three gaps up on three consecutive openings to the completion point at D. This is the market's way of showing us that there is strength to the upside and that the bulls are in control. The bars increase in size with the closing prices at the upper ends of the ranges. This would certainly be a consideration for any trader trying to sell this market short. There is nothing wrong with passing on a setup such as this. A market can always be entered on a retracement pattern or Gartley pattern if necessary. As we can further see in Figure 11.3, the market trends up from this point. There are shallow pullbacks and an acceleration of price to the upside. Had a trader entered on the AB=CD pattern before realizing the warning signs, the trade could be managed as a countertrend trade in trend conditions as outlined in Chapter 10. We do not see tail closes in the CD leg, but the gap-up openings and the wide range bars are sufficient to warrant the trader's attention. All warning signs do not have to be present for the trader to make a trading decision to stand aside or wait for further confirmation.

MONEY MANAGEMENT

Money management is the most important element of a trading plan. It is a function of risk control and, if utilized properly, will allow traders to trade through periods of drawdowns and losing streaks without blowing out their accounts. In order to trade professionally and successfully, you must learn to follow your trading plan, which includes a plan for money management. Money management begins with an attitude: Again, traders must learn to think in terms of probabilities and not certainties. This is particularly true with regard to the patterns we have shown throughout this book, because they have a positive expectation if traded consistently with sound trading principles, including money management.

One important side note on poor money management: Added to the obvious loss of financial resources is the emotional stress that is placed on the trader. This stress can be manifested in the form of depression or addictive behaviors such as alcoholism or drug abuse. To prevent these very destructive behaviors from occurring due to lack of proper money management, traders can set up a structure in their trading to start with good habits such as always using stop-loss orders.

If a real broker is used, an order structure can be implemented so that each time a trade is placed a stop-loss order must also be placed or the broker does not place the order. Electronic trading does not allow for this type of structure, so before beginning trading live with real capital it would be best for traders to commit fully to themselves that they will always use stop-loss orders and never violate a money management rule.

Using a Percentage of Total Trading Capital as Risk

Using a small percentage of total trading capital on any one trade is an excellent way of preventing blowing out an account. We can use an example of a $100,000 trading account to illustrate this point. If the trader were to risk 100 percent of the $100,000 on any one trading idea and lose, he would have brought the account balance to zero in one swift drawdown. If the trader were to risk 50 percent of the account on each of two trades and lose both times, he would have brought the account balance to zero in two trades.

Since trading is a game of probabilities, we know that there will be winning streaks and losing streaks. We do not, however, know in what order they will play out; then it is only logical to structure the money management to allow us to stay in the game long enough to not be blown out of the game by drawdowns that will occur. This is why it is going to be important to always commit only a small percentage of capital to any one trading idea.

We suggest using a risk in the range of 1 percent to 3 percent of total trading capital on any one trade. This will prevent any catastrophic losses on any particular trade. In the example of the $100,000 trading account, using a 1 percent risk or $1,000, the trader has to be wrong 100 times in a row to bring the account balance to zero. Using 3 percent or $3,000, the trader would have to be wrong approximately 33 times in a row to bring the account balance to zero.

Novice traders should certainly use the 1 percent level, and as they gain more experience they could consider using the 3 percent level. We do not believe going above the 3 percent risk of your trading capital on any one trade should ever be implemented. The trade setup may look absolutely foolproof and the trader may believe that it cannot fail; but it is only one trade in many and never worth the risk. There is an old saying in trading: *Never go for broke—you just might get it.*

One of the great benefits of the patterns presented in this book is they can all be traded with the amount of capital at risk, the stop-loss orders, and the profit objectives figured before the pattern completes. Figure 11.4 shows a trade example using 3 percent of the total trading capital at risk and how to determine the number of shares appropriate for the trade. We use a hypothetical $100,000 trading account. Here are the steps to follow to calculate the number of shares for this trade:

1. $100,000 \times 3\% = \$3,000$. This is the total amount of risk for this trade.

2. The entry point is at $37.50 and the stop-loss will be set at $2.00 per share and placed at $35.50.

3. We then take the amount of the stop-loss order, $2.00 in this case, and divide it into the total amount of risk, $3,000 in this trade.

4. $\$3,000 \div \$2.00 = 1,500$. This gives us the number of shares to trade; 1,500 shares can be traded in this setup using a 3 percent risk parameter with a $2.00 per share stop-loss order (1,500 shares stopped out at $2.00 per share equal $3,000).

In this example, the maximum amount the trader can lose is $3,000 or 3 percent of the trading capital. We never want to risk more than 10 percent of a stock's price using a stop-loss order. As an example, if the stock is a $50 stock, we would never risk more than $5.00 as a stop-loss order. Around 5 percent is usually quite reasonable. We have said this several times throughout the book and we will repeat it again here: If the risk is too great in the trade, then pass and find another trade setup with suitable risk.

As discussed and shown in the previous chapters, the exits can be determined using several methods. If we were to use an equal amount of risk ($2.00 in this example), take the first exit at $39.50 per share, and move the stop-loss order to breakeven, this would

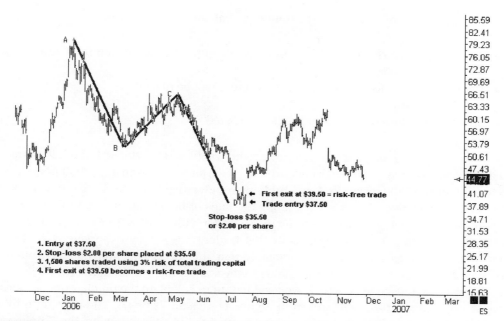

FIGURE 11.4 Calculating the correct number of shares for an AB=CD buy pattern trade setup on a Sandisk Corporation (SNDK) daily chart.

allow us to take a profit that is equal to the original risk in the trade, and moving the stop-loss order to breakeven puts us in a risk-free trade.

- Using 2 percent risk in this trade example, the total amount of capital at risk would be $2,000 and the correct number of shares would be 1,000.
- Using 1 percent risk in this trade example, the total amount of capital at risk would be $1,000 and the correct number of shares would be 500.

Each trader will have a different tolerance level for risk. It is very important to determine ahead of time what your risk tolerance level is.

The trader can calculate for each trade how many shares can be traded. If the account balance is down due to losses, the trader must recalculate downward the percentage of risk being used. If the account balance has increased, the trader can recalculate upward the percentage of risk being used. This ensures that when there is a losing streak the trader is trading fewer shares, and when there is a winning streak the trader can trade more shares. Most important, it prevents traders from devastating their accounts.

Here is a recap of what steps the trader can calculate ahead of time:

- Total amount of risk based on a predetermined percentage of the total amount of trading capital available.
- The use of a stop-loss order; how and where it will be placed.
- The profit targets.
- How the stop-loss order will be moved or trailed.

Now let's look at an example of a trader who wants to trade the S&P E-mini contract and is starting with an account size of $20,000. (We want to make an important point here before looking at this example. Many brokerages advertise low margins for day trading the S&P E-minis, perhaps something along the lines of being able to day trade the S&P E-minis at $1,000 per contract. Based on this, a trader with a $10,000 account might think he could trade 10 contracts. Most likely that trader, unless very experienced, will not survive using that as a money management system. It is inconsequential and has nothing to do with calculating and applying sound money management techniques.)

We can use the same approach we used before to calculate the number of contracts traded using the Gartley sell pattern in Figure 11.5 as an example. The entry into this trade would be at 1405.50 and the stop-loss order would be placed above the X point of

FIGURE 11.5 Example of S&P E-mini 5-minute chart of Gartley sell pattern—calculating the correct number of contracts.

the pattern at 1407.75. This is a stop-loss of 2.25 points or $112.50 per contract. Using a hypothetical $20,000 account, let's calculate the number of contracts using 1 percent risk and assume this is a novice trader:

1. $20,000 × 1% = $200. This is the total amount of risk in the trade.
2. $200 ÷ $112.50 = 1.7. The correct amount of contracts based on this risk profile is 1. You want to round down any uneven numbers.
3. The entry point is 1405.50, and the stop-loss order is placed at 1407.75, which is 2.25 points or $112.50 per contract.
4. We take the amount of risk, $200 in this example, and divide by where the stop-loss order is placed; in this example the correct placement is just above the D point at 1407.75 or 2.25 points.

The maximum amount the trader can lose on this trade is $112.50. Until the account balance is increased to a level that can add on a contract, the trader must plan trades with one exit. There is an advantage to this, and that is the trader will be learning excellent execution skills at this point in his trading. Novice traders are most likely at this point in their trading careers to lose on more trades because they are still gaining market experience. This is the time to keep risk very small and build trading skills.

In this particular example, the trader could use an exit strategy of taking a profit equal to the amount of risk in the trade. In this case that would be at 1403.25, which would provide a $112.50 or 2.25-point profit.

- Using 2 percent risk in this trade example, the total amount of risk would be $400 or three contracts.
- Using 3 percent risk in this trade example, the total amount of risk would be $600 or five contracts.

If the stop-loss order were 5 points or $250, the trader would have to pass on that type of setup and wait for a setup that had an appropriate stop-loss placement based on the percent of risk being used. The risk using a 5-point stop would exceed the $200 maximum allowable loss per trade. It is a mistake to use stops that are too close; this will result in unnecessary losses and frustration on the trader's part. It is an art and a skill learning to place stops correctly.

Each trader needs to decide based on one's risk tolerance profile and trading experience what percentage of capital to risk. An important consideration in this decision is the number of trades the trader has open at one time. The less experienced the trader, the fewer open trades the trader should have. A very hard lesson to learn is watching several open (overtrading) positions turn into losses at the same time.

Traders should take into account a worst-case scenario if trading more than one open position. They should know how much of a drawdown the account would sustain if the worst-case scenario occurred. Our suggestion would be to concentrate on learning one or two patterns in one or two markets and become proficient with them. There will be time to add in more patterns and markets if the trader so chooses.

Here are several trading mistakes that can devastate a trader's account. They are all violations of sound money management practices:

- Not placing stop-loss orders. This allows a small loss to turn into a large loss and is a cardinal sin in trading.
- Overtrading. Here traders are either trading outside of their trading plans, taking random trades, or having too many open positions at one time.
- Moving stop-loss orders to avoid a loss. Never increase a predetermined stop-loss amount.
- Exceeding the amount of capital risked on one trade or multiple open trades.
- Not taking profits when available. This is letting a winning trade turn into a losing trade and should absolutely be avoided.

We leave you with the most important rules at the end of this chapter:

1. Rule #1: Always use stop-loss orders.
2. Rule #2: Never violate Rule #1.

CHAPTER 12

Using Options with the Fibonacci Ratios and Patterns

$\mathbf{T}$ his chapter covers how to use options with extension patterns, such as the Butterfly pattern or the 1.272 and 1.618 extensions. We assume you have some knowledge of options and how they work. If not, we recommend checking out the Chicago Board Options Exchange web site (www.cboe.com). The site is an excellent source of educational material for all levels of options traders, including tutorials that can be downloaded free of charge.

CALL AND PUT OPTIONS DEFINED

The call option gives the buyer, or owner, the right—but not the obligation—to purchase the underlying instrument at a specified price, known as the strike price, for a specified time period (i.e., until the expiration date). The writer of the call option, the one who sells the option, is obligated to sell the underlying instrument at the specified (strike) price if that option is assigned.

The put option gives the owner the right to sell the underlying instrument at a specified price, known as the strike price, within a fixed period of time (i.e., until the expiration date). The writer of the put option, the one who sells the option, is obligated to purchase the underlying instrument from the option buyer if it is assigned.

FACTORS THAT INFLUENCE THE PRICE OF AN OPTION

Many things can contribute to and change the price of an option. Since an option is a derivative of an underlying instrument, its value is directly tied to that underlying instrument, whether it is a stock, commodity, or futures index option. Here are a few of the main variables that will affect the option's price:

- The price of the underlying stock, commodity, or future.
- The strike price—whether it is in-the-money, at-the-money, or out-of-the-money. See Figures 12.1 and 12.2 for examples of all of these.
  - In-the-money refers to a call option that is above the strike price and a put option that is below the strike price.
  - At-the-money refers to a call or put option that is at the strike price.
  - Out-of-the-money refers to a call option where the strike price is above the underlying instrument's price and a put option where the strike price is below the underlying instrument's price.
- The amount of time to the expiration date—time premium is priced into an option, and as the expiration date draws closer the time premium will decay.
- Volatility of the underlying instrument—as a rule of thumb, the higher the volatility, the higher the price of the option.

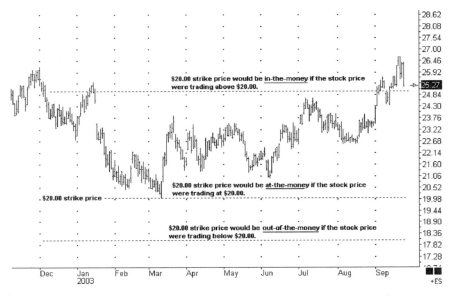

FIGURE 12.1 Microsoft (MSFT) daily chart showing a call option example of at-the-money, in-the-money, and out-of-the-money strike prices.

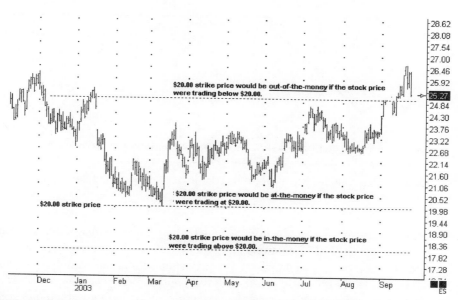

FIGURE 12.2 Microsoft (MSFT) daily chart showing a put option example of at-the-money, in-the-money, and out-of-the-money strike prices.

- Dividend payout of an underlying stock during the lifetime of the option.
- Interest rates, both long-term and short-term, will have an effect on the option's pricing.
- Open interest, or how much interest there is in any particular option at a particular strike price and expiration date. If there is more open interest, then there is likely to be a larger premium priced into the option. The option buyer wants to purchase options that have a fair amount of open interest.

CONTROLLING RISK WITH OPTIONS

There are many ways to use options, but here we will focus on just one simple strategy for each type of option:

- Buy call options when there may be a significant move to the upside based on a longer-term pattern.
- Buy put options when there may be a significant move to the downside based on a longer-term pattern.

Figure 12.3 illustrates when we utilize call options and put options.

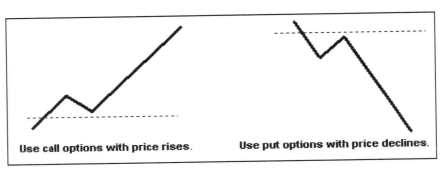

Use call options with price rises.   Use put options with price declines.

FIGURE 12.3 Buy call options when expecting a large rise in prices, and buy put options when expecting a large decline in prices.

The main reason to use options at what may be major or significant market turning points is the leverage they offer. Options can be purchased for a set dollar amount that can be a small portion of trading capital. When a particular market or underlying instrument has a large move in the anticipated direction, option prices can increase dramatically, giving the option investor a potential large return on a relatively small investment.

It is important to understand that about 85 percent or all options expire worthless. Therefore, the trader must risk only a small portion of total trading capital on any one option strategy. When using this option strategy, the trader's risk is limited to the cost of the option. If the trade does not work and the option expires worthless, then the total dollar amount expended for the option purchase is the total loss in the trade. This gives the trader limited risk and a large profit potential. This must be viewed and utilized as part of the trader's overall money management plan.

EXAMPLES OF USING OPTIONS WITH EXTENSION PATTERNS

One of the reasons we like to use options with extension patterns, such as the Butterfly pattern or a 1.272 or 1.618 extension, is that the options generally are marked down in price at that point. In longer time frames, such as daily or weekly charts, patterns generally will have an excessive amount of bullishness or bearishness close to the completion points—bullishness in the case of sell patterns and bearishness in the case of buy patterns. This in itself will generally cause the out-of-the-money options to collapse in premium.

Our strategy is to buy out-of-the-money calls or puts on or near the completion of the pattern. This gives the trade and pattern some time to complete, and we do not have to time an exact entry point in sometimes volatile market conditions. This can be an advantage at times over trading the outright futures or stocks.

We will look at two examples, one a purchase of call options that was a successful trade and one a purchase of put options that expired worthless.

Soybeans Call Option Purchase

Call options are purchased around the completion of the 1.272 extension (shown in Figure 12.4). Soybeans are trading in the 5.50 per bushel area at the end of August, and December out-of-the-money call options at a 600 strike price are purchased for around $2.00 per option or $200 per contract (100 calls). The expiration in December would give the market time to move up.

After being held for over two months with little price action, once the market starts to move up in a trendlike fashion the options increase in value. The same trade management techniques we have covered in earlier chapters can be used with options. The .618 level offers a good first profitable exit point, as the options have gone from out-of-the-money to at-the-money around the 600 strike price. A good trade management technique with options is to sell half of the option contracts once they reach close to double in price. For example, this option contract was purchased at $200; half the options could be sold once the value of the option contract reaches approximately $400 in value. This reduces the risk in the trade, and even if the other half then expires worthless the trade has become risk-free.

Once the price of soybeans reaches the 1.272 extension on the upside, the options then trade in-the-money; with little time left, the value of the options becomes almost all

FIGURE 12.4 Soybeans daily chart of out-of-the-money call options purchased near a 1.272 extension pattern completion.

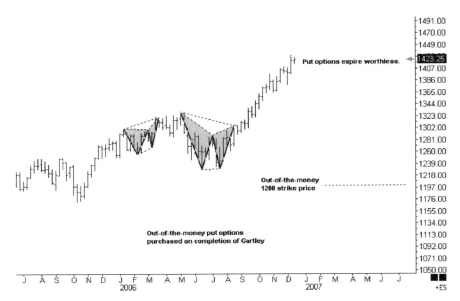

FIGURE 12.5 S&P 500 weekly chart example of put option purchase where options expired worthless.

intrinsic and is close to triple the price paid. The second half of the call options could be sold around the 1.272 extension at a good profit.

S&P 500 Put Option Purchase

This put option trade does not work out as well as the soybeans call option trade. The same basic strategy is used—buy out-of-the-money put options based on longer-term extension patterns. The put options are purchased for around $850 per option contract. The futures index options such as these are generally more expensive than other options, and we try to purchase them below a $1,000 risk level per option contract.

As you can see in Figure 12.5, the extension pattern is the Butterfly pattern, but the options in this trade are purchased near the completion of the first Gartley sell pattern. The assumption is that the Gartley pattern is a retest of the Butterfly pattern highs and the market will then have a larger correction down. However, the market continues to trend up and these options expire worthless.

Always use strict money management when trading options, and risk only a small portion of total trading capital on one option trade. Trading options can be a profitable strategy when used correctly. You can reduce market exposure by not trading the stock, commodity, or future outright through volatile periods. Trading options requires due diligence on the trader's part and an understanding of the nature and pricing of options.

CHAPTER 13

Building a Trading Plan

Developing a sound trading plan is essential to successful trading. The trading plan gives the trader guidelines, rules, focus, and direction. It can greatly aid traders during periods of drawdown or difficult trading times. A trading plan will help the trader identify whether the rough trading times are due to market conditions or to trading errors. The trading plan acts as a rebalancing tool and enables the trader to get back on track to following and executing sound trading principles according to the trading plan.

A well-defined trading plan can help traders to see in black and white what is happening in the internals of their own trading. It allows for an objective view of where the greatest areas of profit come from and how to increase profits. It also allows an objective view of where losses are coming from so as to make adjustments to correct unnecessary losses or losses that are too large in proportion to wins.

As traders, we are always looking for the best tools to help us maximize profits and minimize risk and losses. A trading plan can be one of the best tools we give ourselves to help us achieve both of those goals.

In this chapter we break the trading plan into three components:

1. *Daily trading plan*—defines what and how you will trade.
2. *Business plan*—provides an overall look at expenses of your trading business.
3. *Disaster plan*—looks ahead to act at times of unforeseen events and circumstances.

The trading plan is something that can be changed and be modified over time. Successful trading requires fine-tuning your execution skills as well as your money management. Taking steps early in the process to establish a trading plan will help put the trader on a path of treating trading as a business.

DAILY TRADING PLAN

The depth and extent of a trading plan will depend largely on your current trading skill level. The more in depth your experience and skill level, the more in depth you can develop a trading plan.

For a novice trader, starting with just a few basics would be appropriate. As skill and experience are acquired, the trader can add onto the initial trade plan. This section explains the basics to help you get started.

Basics of a Trading Plan

The most obvious place to start is with what you are trading. Here are several ideas to include as a start:

- Define the markets you will trade.
- Define specific setups you will trade.
- Define entry point triggers into a trade.
- Define market conditions that would void the trade.
- Define the number of shares or contracts to be traded.
- Define how much risk is in the trade by using money management rules.
- Define stop-loss placement.
- Define profit objective targets and how and when a stop-loss order is moved.

Use this list as a checklist until these questions become second nature. One excellent habit to develop is to write the information on a chart of the market that you will be trading. Refer to Figure 13.1 for an example of using a price chart as a checklist for the basic trading plan.

Let's assume that a trader will be trading the S&P E-mini market from a 5-minute time frame and is going to trade all Gartley patterns that form, and the trader has done due diligence in planning how the trades are entered and what conditions prevent the trader from entering a trade. As the pattern is forming and before it reaches the completion point, the trader can write out all information pertaining to the basic trading plan for that pattern in that market. We suggest actually printing out the chart as the pattern is forming and writing in by hand the trading plan for that pattern.

This will accomplish a few important trading goals:

- Keeps the trader focused on what he should be doing and following the trading plan.
- Defines a specific reason for the trade.

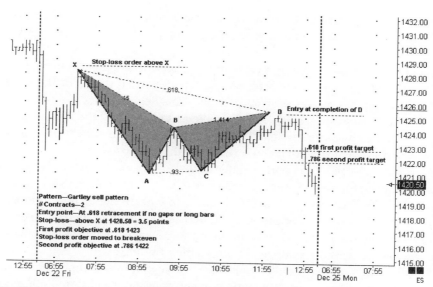

Pattern—Gartley sell pattern
Contracts—2
Entry point—At .618 retracement if no gaps or long bars
Stop-loss—above X at 1428.50 = 3.5 points
First profit objective at .618 1423
Stop-loss order moved to breakeven
Second profit objective at .786 1422

FIGURE 13.1 S&P E-mini 5-minute chart of Gartley sell pattern. Example of using a chart as a trading plan.

- Outlines what actions the trader will take at specific times during the trade and how he will execute the trade management.
- Defines the specific risk the trader must assume for the trade so that he will determine in advance of the trade if the risk is acceptable.

The important part is learning to follow the trading plan. Doing so repetitiously will greatly help you achieve taking one trade after another according to your trading plan.

The exercise will help the trader as the market is moving in real time to follow a specific set of preplanned actions, which will help minimize emotional decisions. If emotional decisions and actions are taken that override the original trading plan, the trader can then use that information in review as a tool for finding specific patterns in the trading that inhibit developing trading skills and growth.

It is easy to look at a static chart in hindsight and see what should have been done. Part of building trading skills is to do this in real time in advance of any trade setups forming, and then have the ability to follow the plan time and time again.

As markets move in real time, price movement can cause all types of mental interference with a trade setup. The more planning and preparation the trader can do before the actual trade, the stronger trading skills he will build. This will also help the trader to learn to think in probabilities.

As you can see, all of the items in the checklist have been addressed in advance of the trade. Taking time to do this will build skills in planning trades, executing trades, and managing trades.

Mark Douglas, author of *Trading in the Zone*, has an excellent exercise to help in developing trading skills and seeing an edge play out with his 20 sample trades exercise.

This exercise has the trader try to execute 20 trades of the same setup without error. In the exercise the trader commits to making a series of 20 trades of the same setup and executes the trades as flawlessly as possible. This helps traders identify flaws in the method or in their execution skills. If they make an error during the 20 trades exercise, they simply refocus on their goal and continue. Refer to Figure 13.2 for a worksheet of the 20 sample trades exercise that can be used for this purpose.

Traders can track the exact performance of the specific patterns they have chosen to trade and are using for each 20 sample trades exercise. This enables them to gauge and measure in objective terms how closely they are following the actual performance of that setup compared to their own performance. If there is a large difference between how the setup performs and the actual outcome of their performance, then they can begin to take steps to stay on par with the setup according to their trading plan.

This will allow traders to look inside their trading and determine important information such as exiting early, entering late, moving stops incorrectly, and other common trading errors that interfere with developing finely tuned trading skills. It is an excellent way to pinpoint problem areas so that corrective measures can be taken to improve performance.

An example would be if 20 trades were completed and the actual performance of the setup yielded +50 S&P E-mini points, but the trader yielded only +15 S&P E-mini points because of trading errors; that gives the trader important information to work with. The trader can now take steps to work on whichever areas need improvement to close that gap.

Take note of the quote that is at the top of the worksheet: "All traders give themselves exactly what they feel they deserve. Trading is an exercise in accumulating money. Once we have learned how to trade (perceive opportunity and execute our trades), who else or what else could be responsible for how much we end up with in our equity account?"—Mark Douglas.

Tracking Performance

As we have discussed, building a trading plan will teach traders to keep focused on what they are supposed to be doing and focused on the process of trading. Adding to the trading plan statistics on the trader's performance is extremely beneficial. When you think about it, how could a trader identify problem areas or evaluate true strengths without some system for doing so? Each trader should have a system that collects objective data on trading performance. It would be hard to imagine a scientist not collecting and analyzing data in order to complete a scientific experiment.

"*All traders give themselves exactly what they feel they deserve. Trading is an exercise in accumulating money. Once we have learned how to trade (perceive opportunity and execute our trades), who else or what else could be responsible for how much we end up with in our equity account?*"

— *Mark Douglas*

	Date	Market	Win	Loss	Scratch	Points
1	/					
2	/					
3	/					
4	/					
5	/					
6	/					
7	/					
8	/					
9	/					
10	/					
11	/					
12	/					
13	/					
14	/					
15	/					
16	/					
17	/					
18	/					
19	/					
20	/					
Notes:						

FIGURE 13.2 Twenty Sample Trades Worksheet.
Source: Mark Douglas, *Trading in the Zone* (New York: New York Institute of Finance/Prentice Hall, 2000).

Athletes focus and collect their performance data on a continuous basis. Traders must come to realize that because trading is a performance-based arena with many components contributing to success or failure, each piece of data is important and will contribute to the success or failure of that trader.

In real time many things can happen quickly that can contribute to profits or losses. Each action the trader takes will contribute to either the profit side or the loss side. At the end of the day, week, or month, it is easy for the trader to overlook important information that contributed to either profit or loss.

The trader may not remember or may rationalize a random trade or other trading errors that keenly affected performance. It is vital that traders have some system of monitoring their own performance. It is also important to learn correct habits that build strengths and eliminate weaknesses. Creating a system to accomplish this will only benefit the trader. This can be accomplished by recognizing what is traded according to the trading plan and what trades or actions do not fall into the trading plan.

It is an unfortunate reality in trading that even trading errors can make a profit. These instances will reinforce very bad trading habits. These types of wins will instill a sense of false confidence. They wrongly tell the trader that if it worked once it will work again. This is usually not the case, and eventually the trader will pay the price.

Keeping track of performance can give the trader an objective view of what needs adjustment. *It is an opportunity to improve performance.* We refer you to *Trading Risk* by Kenneth L. Grant and *Enhancing Trader Performance* by Brett N. Steenbarger; these are both guides to setting up this information.

Using Trader Performance Statistics

A situation that could occur within the trader's statistics that could be unidentified and overlooked may be something like the trader achieving a 70 percent wins record on total trades for a one-month period but still losing money. This could be evidence that there is a problem with controlling losses or a tendency to taking profits too soon before the trade plan calls for it, or a combination of both. It could also be evidence that there are random trades occurring that are not profitable and are eating away at the profits of the trading plan. Whatever the case may be, it is imperative that the trader look inside his trading to determine the cause so that a solution may be applied.

Statistics may also uncover a problem with overtrading. The number of trades per day, week, and month could help the trader identify a problem in this area and then find a solution. Having a system to match up what they *are* trading compared with what they *should be* trading will greatly aid traders in fine-tuning their trading skills.

Another example could be giving away profits. If traders find that profits are given away frequently at particular times of day, it may help them to establish that they need work identifying a trend occurring if the losses are countertrend trades initiated during a trend.

There are many areas that the trader can become aware of and benefit greatly from by keeping statistics on performance. Here are some basic ideas to start with that can easily be put into spreadsheet format. Traders can start with as much as they feel is necessary and appropriate to their current skill level.

- Win/loss ratio (number of wins divided by number of losses).
- Number of trades per day.
- Number of contracts or shares.
- Number of wins.
- Number of losses.
- Number of scratched trades.

They can be broken down further by:

- Number of wins—long trades.
- Number of losses—long trades.
- Number of wins—short trades.
- Number of losses—short trades.
- Number of scratched trades—long trades.
- Number of scratched trades—short trades.

Determining the dollar amounts of wins and losses is important:

- Dollar wins.
- Dollar losses.
- Dollar average win per share or contract.
- Dollar average loss per share or contract.

Some other items that the trader can easily keep track of include:

- Number of consecutive wins.
- Number of consecutive losses.
- Number of consecutive win days.
- Number of consecutive loss days.
- Average profit per trade.
- Average loss per trade.

Keeping track of trader performance statistics will uncover patterns that otherwise would be impossible to see. For example, a trader might maintain a steady record of 65 percent wins and then suddenly drop down to 50 percent; the trader then has information on where to look for the cause of the sudden change.

Another pattern could be a trader who maintains profitability at a steady 65 percent to 70 percent win record but then incurs a larger than usual loss one month with the same win/loss ratio. On the flip side, the trader's win record might drop down to 50 percent one month but still remain profitable.

All of the information can be used to determine what traders are doing correctly and what errors are being made so that they can make changes. This type of information can also alert the trader to a change in market environment that may warrant adjustments to the original trading plan. If there is no system incorporated into the trading plan to determine this, then it will be unlikely anything will be changed in the long run, good or bad.

TRADING AS A BUSINESS

Trading is a business and should be approached as such. There are costs associated with learning to trade and with actual trading. An individual should carefully look at this before venturing into trading.

Taking a business approach and doing some planning in this area will help you evaluate the associated costs. We take a look in this section at some of the costs that are associated with trading. We also look at extending the trading plan to incorporate an annual business plan for those traders who are ready to move into that area.

Trading Education

Although there are exceptions, learning to trade at a level of profitability to make a living will require a solid trading education and time. It can require a considerable amount of money to explore many types of trading methodologies before traders find one that suits their personality that they evolve into their own unique trading style.

It would make sense for traders to formulate a plan around how they want to approach their education in learning to trade. There are many ways to explore learning different methods of trading, including:

- Live workshops and seminars.
- Trade shows.
- Books, magazines, and newspapers.
- Web sites.
- Live trading rooms.
- Mentoring and tutoring programs.
- Newsletters.

It is likely that over the course of a learning curve a beginning trader will explore several of these categories in combination. The trader should investigate each and evaluate the cost and possibly plan a budget around this. For instance, the trader may decide to set aside $3,000 to $5,000 the first year to use for expenses associated with a trading education. It could be allocated to attending a live workshop or seminar, joining a live trading room, studying books, and taking out magazine subscriptions. Each year the education costs can be reevaluated based on where the trader is in the learning curve and what education is needed at that point.

If the trader chooses to attend live trading events, there will most likely be travel costs associated with those events that should also be taken into consideration.

We are often asked, "How long will it take to learn to trade successfully?" This is not a question that can be answered with any specific time frame. There are many variables to be considered, such as:

- The amount of time the trader can commit to learning, studying, and practicing trading.
- How well the trader can outline and follow a trading plan.
- How much previous experience the trader may have; this can either contribute to or take away from the learning curve if there are bad habits that need to be broken and relearned.

Experience is one thing that cannot be taught. All elements and components of a proven solid trading methodology can be taught, but experience must be gained by the individual trader. Traders who have time to experience markets and trading on a regular basis will absorb more experience than a trader who has limited time. Additional planning a trader could do is develop a time line to a goal and then plan the steps necessary to reach that goal.

A word of caution here: Each step in the trading education is important and has a purpose and a place. Do not overlook the challenges and rewards of taking each step. We have not yet come across any "fast road to profits" system in trading; success will require hard work, perseverance, and commitment on the trader's part.

Software, Computer, and Office Costs

Traders must decide what charting program(s) to use that will best suit their needs. There are many available, and attending trade shows can be an excellent way to view them and evaluate their performance. This is another area of expense that any trader must incur and plan for.

Along with a charting program, the trader must also evaluate computer equipment and make sure to use an appropriate computer system with the software. This can also add to the initial costs associated with trading. Here is a list of items to evaluate and plan for as an expense of setting up a trading business:

- Computer equipment.
- Monitors; multiple monitors may be necessary.
- Software program/programs.
- Data providers for charting packages.
- Brokerage/commission costs.
- Internet access.
- Telephone equipment.
- Copy machine.
- Fax machine.
- Office supplies.

Traders new to trading should investigate what it will cost them to run their business on a monthly and annual basis. This will help them gauge realistically how much they must clear each month/year to make a living in the trading business.

Annual Business Plan

The end of each year is a time to prepare for the coming year with the trading plan and a business plan. The trading plan can be reviewed from the previous year and adjustments made for the coming year. The business plan will encompass the basic trading plan.

Maybe there were some markets that were not successful, and traders may reevaluate their approaches to those markets by looking at the internal data they collected throughout the year in their trading statistics. An evaluation of the specific trade management of specific patterns may reveal approaches that can be adjusted.

It is a time to take stock and prepare for the next year's trading. The trader can evaluate any changes to the basic approach and specific trade management issues. Here are some things to evaluate and plan for on an annual basis:

- Which markets will be traded in the coming year.
- A trading plan for each market.
- Time frames traded.
- A plan for incrementally adding on shares or contracts.
- Specific trading issues to study and improve or focus on (e.g., learning a new strategy, improving money management, trader psychology, etc.).
- An outline of how the trader will stay on track and focused throughout the year. This could encompass lifestyle changes or scheduled reviews of the trading plan to evaluate whether the trader is staying on track.

- A mission statement for the coming year.
- A review of trading expenses for the past year and a forecast for the coming year.
- Creation of goals and a plan on how to achieve those goals.

This process of trading does not have to be complicated or overwhelming and should be suited to the trader's experience level. Involving yourself in this area of trading will sharpen the focus and create a well-thought-out road map of where and how to reach your goals as a trader.

Traders are continually in a state of uncertainty when involved in and trading real-time markets. Even on occasions when the trader is very off the track and not trading according to plan, the trading plan is a tool to get back to developing good trading habits. Having a well-defined plan is a way for traders to have some grounding and, in a sense, some security, in that they can always refocus on the basics and move on from there.

DISASTER PLANS

The Chicago Mercantile Exchange has a slogan: "Where there is no such thing as no such thing." This sums up why you need to create some sort of disaster plan. This part of the trading plan will entail thinking out as many what-if scenarios as possible. If you encounter an extreme event that you had not considered, then do the best you can based on the scenarios you have thought of.

If you trade long enough, it is not a matter of *if* some type of disaster will occur, but a matter of *when* some type of disaster will occur. These times can either benefit the trader to an extreme or devastate the trader to an extreme. With any luck, it may be a neutral outcome. Many of the unexpected occurrences can be dealt with if the trader has thought ahead and planned for these types of incidents.

Many types of professions train intensively for unexpected and rare occurrences. Almost anyone in medical fields such as doctors, nurses, and EMT personnel train for emergencies. Airline pilots and crews are mandated by the federal government to have specific annual hours of recurrent training to handle every imaginable type of unexpected event. Firefighters, police and specialized units of the police forces, as well as military personnel and all of those specialized forces train hour upon hour to handle stressful on-the-job situations. The approach and reasoning are really quite simple: If an individual has had the benefit of training, practicing and rehearsing through drills, then in a situation that is sudden and likely to cause high stress, fear, or anxiety that individual will be prepared to act. That is very important; trained individuals keep their wits about them, do not panic, and are able to act under unexpected, extreme stress.

It will be a great advantage to any trader to take some time to plan for what-if situations. Unprepared traders have been known to have a "deer in the headlights" response and literally freeze up both physically and mentally at the precise time they need to take action.

There is a syndrome that people can succumb to under extreme duress known as "negative panic." The person goes into a type of shock and is not able to comprehend what is happening, does not realize there is an emergency, and can even feel a sense of euphoria that nothing is wrong. It is our brains' way of protecting us at times when our systems go through sudden and severe shocks.

Training yourself to think and act under excessive pressure is part of trading. Traders take on uncertainty each day they trade and become accustomed to normal trading days and routines. It will be the skilled and prepared trader who will be able to take action during rarer incidents of extreme uncertainty.

Some types of unexpected events that have occurred in the past include the Federal Reserve raising or lowering interest rates without notice during market hours. This can cause markets to move extremely fast and can catch almost all market participants off guard. The bond and currency markets can spike more than two full points in a matter of seconds in this type of environment. A trader who is on the wrong side of that move and did not use stop-loss protection will surely suffer serious losses as well as psychological damage.

The attack on the World Trade Center in New York City on September 11, 2001, is an example of an extreme outlier event that closed the markets for several days. When the markets reopened on September 17, 2001, there was a panicked sell-off for five days followed by a rally that lasted for several months. On reopening, the market gapped down almost 60 points in the S&P 500 contract. It is easy to see that anyone who had been long on the closing was met with large losses on the reopen. (See Figure 13.3.)

Unexpected news announcements, political events worldwide, terrorist actions, and technical meltdowns can all cause the most extreme sudden moves in the markets. Markets do not like uncertainty and will react violently at times with extreme cases of uncertainty.

One very important trading rule to follow that will help to minimize damage done by events that are beyond your control is: *Never violate money management rules in position sizing or use of stop-loss orders*. In rare market moves caused by unexpected events, it is quite probable that your stop-loss order will be filled at a worse price. This is something that is unavoidable and can and will happen. The best thing to do is to be thankful you indeed had a stop-loss order, brush yourself off, and keep going.

On the other side of the coin, if you happen to find yourself on the right side of one of these sudden moves, consider it a gift and take it. These moves can reverse as quickly as they originated, and if you find you have a windfall profit the best thing to do is to take it quickly.

Along with these types of rare occurrences, the trader can plan for other types of potential disasters. These items involve some thought and planning ahead of time, but if

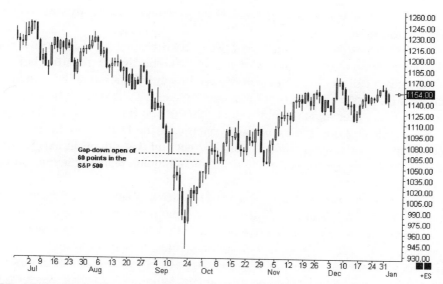

FIGURE 13.3 S&P 500 daily chart. The markets closed on September 11, 2001, and reopened on September 17 with a gap-down open of 60 points in the S&P 500.

and when they occur it will be well worth the additional time spent. We list some of the more common types of things that can play havoc with a trading day:

- *Power outages.* It is good to make sure your cell phone is charged at all times in case you need to call in orders during a power outage. Telephones and Internet services can frequently go out with electrical outages. It is a good policy if day trading to close out any open positions if they cannot be properly managed. Some traders have wireless connections on laptop computers and can utilize those during a power outage.

- *Computer crashes.* Know in advance what your plan is if you cannot manage open positions and do not have access to data in the event of your computer crashing. Technology is not perfect, and it will fail at the most inopportune time.

- *Order entry errors.* Occasionally traders will incorrectly enter the wrong number of shares of contracts for an order. It is not wise if the order is beyond your money management plan to try to gain a profit. Remember, you can gain a larger loss just as easily. Close out the excess number of shares or contracts immediately, and go on with the trade as planned.

- *Entering incorrect buy or sell orders.* Another form of an order entry error is when a trader enters a buy order instead of a sell order. It is a very good habit to get into to check what any open position is upon any order being filled. There are many stories of traders who at the end of the day thought they had a profit from their trades only to find out it was a loss because the orders were entered incorrectly and no check of positions was done.

- *Incorrect information on a statement.* Keep good trading records. Occasionally it will happen that something shows up in your account that you neither bought nor sold. Usually a call to the broker will resolve this. It is imperative that traders keep good daily records, including order numbers for each fill. It does not take much time to jot down an order number, and it is usually the first thing a trading desk will ask for. Before closing the trading platform each day, the trader should meticulously check to make sure any open orders are correct and that the profit/loss for the day matches the trader's records. This in itself will eliminate many difficulties in resolving errors.
- *Unexpected news announcements/exchange closures.* An exchange closing suddenly happens occasionally and can be due to technical problems at the exchange or to world events as we saw on September 11, 2001. Occasionally, unexpected news announcements will severely move a market. It has happened in the past that any orders in a market at a particular exchange have been canceled. It is possible to hedge the position by using another instrument at another exchange. As an example, traders who are open a short position in the S&P E-mini market could go long the Dow futures. At times like these the phone lines at brokers and trading desks will be very hectic, and it may be difficult to get through. If it is not possible to hedge the position and the market reopens at a disadvantage, get out as gracefully as you can and move on. Remember, these are rare occurrences that you have no control over, and you do the best you can.
- *Large gap openings.* If you hold positions overnight, sooner or later you will have a market open beyond your stop-loss on a gap opening. Gap openings happen when there is an imbalance of buyers and sellers and can occur when some type of news item comes out overnight that impacts that market or stock. If this happens, it can be handled by waiting about 20 minutes after the open of that market. If the price then moves in your favor, place a stop-loss order at the high or low. If the price continues to move in your favor, you can either trail the stop or exit around your original stop-loss order if the price reaches it. If the gap was in your favor, it is wise to take at least part of the windfall and adjust the stop. Many times news announcements that move a market suddenly will reverse, and you do not want to be in a position to give back profits. If the price then continues at a loss, you will be stopped out at the high or low at which you placed the stop-loss order.
- *High levels of stress or distractions.* Each trader has a different tolerance for stress and distractions. There will be times in each person's life that an unusual amount of stress or outside distractions will make it difficult to trade efficiently. Some types of stresses that fit into this are divorce or relationship problems, death of a loved one, and illness. Once again, take some time to plan ahead with regard to what actions are best to take, such as stopping or limiting trading until some balance is restored.

It is very easy to lose money trading during times of excessive stress, and most often taking a break is the best solution.

SUMMARY

Trading is a process of constant refinements and adjustments. Taking time to outline each part of an overall trading plan will allow traders to make adjustments as they move forward in their trading.

The actual daily trading plan can be adjusted as a trader sees shifts in market conditions. Changes with trade management can be made as the trader becomes more experienced or when conditions warrant. In the long term, this will help to increase profits and reduce losses when necessary. Without any type of daily trading plan, it will be almost impossible for a trader to determine where areas are that need changing and improvement. The time frame each trader works from will determine how often adjustments are made. It may be necessary to make adjustments and refinements more frequently on shorter time frames versus longer time frames.

The business plan portion can be reviewed monthly, quarterly, or every six months to evaluate whether the cost of the trading business is in line with the plan. At these review points, traders can determine if they are covering their costs. Any adjustments can be made to this that they deem necessary. Commissions are a trading expense that traders may want to evaluate as a cost of their business; they can shop for better commissions or consult their broker for a lower commission if necessary.

As different scenarios arise that fit under the disaster plan category, traders can make adjustments as to how to handle those situations. They may experience a condition that they find an acceptable way of handling, and should make a note of it for future reference. However, if a situation arises that they are not prepared for and they need help with solutions, they can ask other traders how they have handled a similar situation in the past. It's very helpful to communicate with other traders and find out in advance ideas for handling the unexpected. Preparing and planning in advance which actions to take in all aspects of trading will keep the trader focused, able to take action, and as calm as possible during both normal trading and the rare occasions when unexpected incidents occur.

There is no right or wrong way to format each of these segments of the overall trading plan. Some traders prefer to write out each segment by hand. Other traders prefer to use spreadsheets or a computer word processing program. It really makes no difference; the important thing is that the trader considers each aspect as a serious and well-thought-out venture and takes time to develop the trading plan.

Combining the three segments of an overall trading plan will strengthen the trader's confidence, increase trading skills, and help the trader learn to operate trading as a business.

CHAPTER 14

Daily Routines

D eveloping routines is an important part of trading preparation. Each trader eventually develops his or her own unique routine. We can think of routines as a checklist for trading. They give us an opportunity to review our past trades, prepare for upcoming trades, and adjust our focus and mental attitude. Routines can balance us at times of uncertainty in the markets and keep us in tune with our trading.

In this chapter we cover three areas that traders can use to develop routines:

1. Trade preparation
2. Mental preparation
3. Physical preparation

There is no right or wrong way to develop a routine, and most traders find their routines evolve as they evolve as traders.

TRADE PREPARATION

Everyone involved in the process of trading should strive to build good habits. Weaving one strand a day of good habits will eventually build an unbreakable cable. Someone who takes the time to prepare for trading is much more likely to succeed than one who spends little or no time and shows up just as the market is opening.

Trade preparation as a routine can be broken down into trade preparation before the market open, during market hours, and after the market close. We will start with premarket preparation.

Premarket Trade Preparation

Premarket Trade Checklist

► Review the markets and/or individual stocks in the overnight markets.

► Review relevant news items released overnight.

► If trading stocks, check for earnings dates and if earnings have been released check the impact on the stock price prior to the market open.

► Check for any economic reports released before the market open. Many times these will have an impact on market prices.

► Review trading plan; if a market or stock is likely to have a gap open that could affect the original trading plan, adjustments may need to be made prior to the open.

► Print out account statements from the day before; review these for any errors.

► Check account to verify any open positions starting the day.

► Check the amount of capital available for trading.

► Set price alerts on charts for pattern completion areas or for stop alerts or profit objectives.

We find it helpful to keep a notebook for writing down market observations that may pertain to the next day's trading and then review the notebook prior to the next day's open. As an example, specific areas of support or resistance can be noted as well as any patterns that may complete the next day or that the trader wants to keep track of. Any observations made should be written down so that the trader can refer back to them when necessary (it is very easy to forget an important observation made while the market is moving).

During Market Hours

During Market Hours Checklist

► Monitor patterns, prices, and open trades. Have patience to wait for your trades to set up. Try to avoid watching each tick unless you are a very short-term trader. Watching each downtick and uptick can wreak havoc on a trader's mental well-being and can be the cause of impulsive trades. Set audio alerts when possible.

► Note any observations on prices or patterns that you want to review later.

► Take frequent breaks during market hours.

► Online chat rooms can be excellent learning tools, but beware of entering trades that are not part of your trading plan or trading setups that you have not studied for yourself.

► Close out any day trades before the close. Do not turn a losing day trade into a position trade by holding it overnight.

If you trade on a short-term time frame such as a 5-minute chart, then it could be part of your trading plan to watch for specific patterns to form throughout the day on that time frame. In that case, the trader would need to monitor the prices in that market throughout the day. However, if the trader is making trades from a longer-term time frame such as a 60-minute or daily chart, then it would not make sense for the trader to watch the prices intently throughout the day.

Many markets now trade almost 24 hours a day, and traders should focus on the markets they want to trade that fit into their daily regimen. Traders who trade on a part-time basis should also choose markets and time frames that do not greatly interfere with their main profession.

After Market Hours

After Market Hours Checklist

► *Always* check accounts before closing trading platforms to ensure any open positions are correct and that closed positions are closed.

► Check the profit/loss in the account against your intraday trading records.

► Check to ensure the number of contracts or shares traded is correct.

► Record all order numbers and trade transactions. See Figure 14.1 for an order sheet example.

► Update spreadsheets for keeping trading data.

► Update any hand charts or other data.

► Note any trading opportunities for the next day; this is the time to do general homework to prepare for the next day's trading. This would include scanning markets and individual stocks for patterns.

► Evaluate any open positions to determine stop-loss orders, profit targets, and so on.

Doing some type of hand charting—drawing graphs or patterns—is an excellent part of any trader's routine. We like to draw a 5-minute chart of that day's S&P 500 market and note the time of day the highs and lows were made, patterns that developed,

	A	B	C	D	E	F	G	H	I	J	K	L
1						Trade Tracking Sheet						
2		Date	Market/Stock	Long/Short	Quantity	Order #	Price	Stop	Exit	Profit	Loss	Commission
3	1											
4	2	17-Jan	ES	Short		2	347658	1441	1446	1443	3		
5	3							1439	1439	5		9.5
6	4	18-Jan	ES	Short		2	458921	1435	1438	1434	1		
7	5							1435	1433.5	1.5		9.5
8	6											
9	7											
10	8											
11	9											
12	10											
13	11											
14	12											
15	13											
16	14											

Sheet1 / Sheet2 / Sheet3 /

FIGURE 14.1 Example of a trade tracking sheet with order number entries.

and any other observations. Refer to Figure 14.2 for an example of a hand chart from the S&P E-mini 5-minute chart. This keeps us alert as to when changes occur and to developing patterns. We believe doing some work by hand each day makes a better connection in the brain and builds an intuitive sense of price patterns. We would like to strongly encourage all traders to include some form of hand charting in their daily routines.

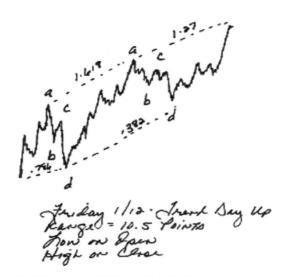

FIGURE 14.2 Example of 5-minute S&P E-mini hand chart.

MENTAL PREPARATION

You want to incorporate into your daily routine methods for preparing mentally for the day's trading and also to access whether you are prepared to trade on any particular day. Here are some items to review each day:

- Have you had enough rest?
- Are you free of circumstances outside of trading that might contribute to high levels of stress?
- Has routine trade preparation been done and have trading plans been prepared?
- Do your senses feel sharp, not under any lingering adverse effects? We recommend consuming no alcohol on days before trading days.
- Are you willing to accept a loss? Sometimes just asking yourself this question will provide the answer to whether you should be trading that day.

Being mentally prepared for trading each day is as important as being prepared with a trading plan. It can be very expensive to attempt to trade when you are not mentally ready to do so. There is nothing wrong with sitting out a trading day or two. Any of the listed items may affect the outcome of a trading day in a negative way.

It can cause further damage mentally to the trader to be left at the end of a day with large losses because of needless trading errors caused by mental errors. In many cases it would be less expensive and better for the overall mental health of the trader to take the day off and go enjoy an activity outside of trading. A series of trading errors can be a warning flag to traders that they need a longer break and should consider taking a few days off, if not more.

As we gain experience as traders, we can learn to gauge our mental ability to do all that is required for good trade execution. We can sense when we are in good mental form and when we are not. We learn to know the point where we cross over a mental boundary. These are times that serious damage can be done to our psyches and our accounts. It is important for each trader to learn where this mental balance is and respect it. A novice trader may find the boundary narrower than that of a trader with more market experience. A more experienced trader is better able to bounce back from losses. Understand that this, too, is a process of expanding your mental capacity to handle all types of trading situations. As you gain experience, the capacity to handle more will increase.

There are actions a trader can take to create a positive mental attitude prior to trading and to focus on thinking in probabilities. Reading a few pages of a motivational book or article can be extremely helpful. One of our favorites is Mark Douglas's *Trading in the Zone*. Douglas speaks to the trader from the heart, and with each sentence the trader feels as though Douglas is speaking directly to him.

Writing a few short phrases or quotes the trader can read and reread throughout the day can help keep the trader focused and in the correct frame of mind. Having trading partners or friends to share trading ideas and stories with can be very helpful. Sometimes just getting it off your chest after a bad day is all that is needed to get back on track and see things with clarity again.

A series of losses can begin to chip away at a trader's mental attitude. Remember that losses will always be a part of trading. A series of losses is most commonly followed by a series of wins. A good way to maintain a positive mental attitude is to understand this and move on to the next trade. Losses tell you that the position is wrong and the stop-loss order prevents a reasonable loss from turning into a devastating loss. There is no reason to take losses personally; if you find you are taking losses personally, then refocus on thinking in probabilities.

A positive mental attitude is as important to traders, if not more so, than any tested method, software program, or indicator they will ever use. There are many motivational books that can be included in the trader's library that encourage a positive mental attitude. A few that we like are:

Think and Grow Rich, by Napoleon Hill.

As a Man Thinketh, by James Allen.

Light from Many Lamps, by Lillian Watson.

Essentials of Trading: It's Not WHAT You Think, It's HOW You Think, by Larry Pesavento and Leslie Jouflas.

We have listed other books in the recommended reading section in the back of the book, and we encourage all readers to investigate many of these fine books.

We would like you to remember this from Winston Churchill's famous speech that he gave at Harrow School during World War II when London was being bombed daily. He said, "Never give in. Never, never, never, never—in nothing, great or small, large or petty—never give in."

PHYSICAL PREPARATION

There is no doubt that being physically fit increases energy, lowers stress, and improves our mental attitudes. All of these things contribute to improved trading skills. It will benefit the trader to include in their routines regular exercise and nutritional eating habits.

Trading can be stressful, and it is wise to prepare our minds and bodies as much as possible to handle the stressful times of trading. Adding exercise into our routines help us to reduce stress that has been brought on by a trading day. Exercise refreshes us so that we see things in a new light. Cardiovascular exercise increases blood flow and releases endorphins that improves our mood and relieves stress.

We mentioned previously the importance of restraining from using any alcohol during the week prior to trading days. Alcohol slows the brain functions and can linger in the system for up to 24 hours. We need to be alert when trading, and certainly overuse of alcohol or drugs will not contribute to a high performance level.

Here are some suggestions to include in your routines:

- *Rest.* A consistent sleep schedule and adequate rest can be very conducive to trading. Try to go to bed at the same time each day and get up at the same time each morning.
- *Nutrition.* Eat a healthy diet and drink plenty of water. Sugar in foods and beverages cause energy levels to drop, which may lead to lack of focus and trading errors. Many foods contribute to maintaining high energy levels and good concentration.
- *Exercise.* Exercise at least three times a week. There are many exercise programs and options to choose from, such as yoga, walking, Pilates, running, weight lifting, and combinations of those.
- *Reduction of distractions.* Distractions can be costly in trading, especially if you are day trading. Taking phone calls can draw focus away from open trades that need immediate attention. Excessive noise can interfere with trading, as can many other outside distractions. Know what level of distractions you can tolerate, and cut out the rest. Chat rooms can be a distraction; choose one where education and learning are the main focus.
- *Time away from trading.* Routinely planning some time away from trading is crucial. Trading can place many demands on us and can be all-consuming. Schedule short breaks and long breaks from trading.

Most traders find that once they have established a solid routine for themselves they may feel off balance, even a bit out of control, if for one reason or another they are not able to follow the routine. This could be something like getting home late before a trading day and not having adequate time to review and accomplish all items on the list for the next day's trading. Once back in the routine, the trader usually feels a sense of familiarity and is back in control. Routines center us amidst an environment of uncertainty.

Sometimes being away from trading for a few days or weeks can give traders a sense of disorientation, of not having their finger on the pulse of the market. Returning after a longer period away from trading and resuming an established routine will usually put them right back where they had left off. Take time to establish a well-thought-out routine that benefits your trading, mental attitude, and physical health.

Useful Resources

There are many great books available for traders—too many to list here. These are some that we feel are most worth taking the time to read. We also include trading magazine sources as well as web site information.

TECHNICAL BOOKS

Bulkowski, Thomas N., *Encyclopedia of Chart Patterns* (New York: John Wiley & Sons, 2000).

Garrett, William, *Investing for Profit with Torque Analysis of Stock Market Cycles* (Englewood Cliffs, NJ: Prentice-Hall, 1973).

Gartley, H.M., *Profits in the Stock Market* (Pomeroy, WA: Lambert-Gann Publishing, 1935).

Gilmore, Bryce, *Geometry of Markets* (Self-published, 1989).

Grant, Kenneth L., *Trading Risk: Enhanced Profitability through Risk Control* (Hoboken, NJ: John Wiley & Sons, 2004).

Hill, John, George Pruitt, and Lundy Hill, *The Ultimate Trading Guide* (New York: John Wiley & Sons, 2000).

Nison, Steve, *Beyond Candlesticks* (New York: John Wiley & Sons, 1994).

Nison, Steve, *Japanese Candlestick Charting Techniques* (New York: New York Institute of Finance, 1991).

Pesavento, Larry, *Fibonacci Ratios with Pattern Recognition* (Greenville, SC: Traders Press, 1997).

Pesavento, Larry, and Peggy MacKay, *The Opening Price Principle* (Greenville, SC: Traders Press, 2000).

Schabacker, R.W., *Stock Market Theory and Practice* (n.p.: B.C. Forbes Publishing Company, 1930).

MOTIVATIONAL BOOKS

Allen, James, *As a Man Thinketh* (Mount Vernon, NY: Peter Pauper Press, 1960).

Bristol, Claude M., *The Magic of Believing* (New York: Pocket Books/Simon & Schuster, 1969).

Hill, Napoleon, *Think and Grow Rich* (New York: Tarcher Publishing, 2005).

LeFèvre, Edwin, *Reminiscences of a Stock Operator* (New York: John Wiley & Sons, 1993).

Longstreet, Roy, *Viewpoints of a Commodity Trader* (Greenville, SC: Traders Press, 1967).

Mack, Gary, with David Casstevens, *Mind Gym* (New York: Contemporary Books/McGraw-Hill, 2001).

Pesavento, Larry, and Leslie Jouflas, *Essentials of Trading; It's Not WHAT You Think, It's HOW You Think* (Greenville, SC: Traders Press, 2004).

Schwartz, Marty, *Pit Bull* (New York: HarperBusiness, 1998).

Smitten, Richard, *The Amazing Life of Jesse Livermore* (Greenville, SC: Traders Press, 1999).

Watson, Lillian, *Light from Many Lamps* (New York: Simon & Schuster, 1951).

INTERVIEWS WITH TRADERS

Collins, Art, *When Supertraders Meet Kryptonite* (Greenville, SC: Traders Press, 2002).

Schwager, Jack, *Market Wizards* (New York: New York Institute of Finance, 1989).

Schwager, Jack, *The New Market Wizards* (New York: HarperBusiness, 1992).

Schwager, Jack, *Stock Market Wizards* (New York: HarperBusiness, 2001).

TRADING PSYCHOLOGY BOOKS

Douglas, Mark, *The Disciplined Trader* (New York: New York Institute of Finance, 1990).

Douglas, Mark, *Trading in the Zone* (New York: New York Institute of Finance/Prentice Hall, 2000).

Kiev, Ari, *Hedge Fund Masters* (Hoboken, NJ: John Wiley & Sons, 2005).

Maltz, Maxwell, M.D., F.I.C.S., *Psycho-Cybernetics* (Englewood Cliffs, NJ: Prentice-Hall, 1960).

McCall, Richard D., *The Way of the Warrior Trader* (New York: McGraw-Hill, 1997).

Murphy, Shane, and Doug Hirschhorn, *The Trading Athlete* (New York: John Wiley & Sons, 2001).

Phillips, Larry W., *Tao of Poker* (Avon, MA: Adams Media Corporation, 2003).

Steenbarger, Brett N., *Enhancing Trader Performance* (Hoboken, NJ: John Wiley & Sons, 2007).

Steenbarger, Brett N., *The Psychology of Trading* (Hoboken, NJ: John Wiley & Sons, 2003).

Sun Tzu, *The Art of War*, trans. Thomas Cleary (Boston: Shambhala Publications, 1991).

TRADING MAGAZINES

Active Trader

Futures Magazine

Technical Analysis of Stocks and & Commodities

Trader Monthly

Trader's Journal

SOFTWARE SOURCES WITH FIBONACCI TOOLS

Ensign Software—www.ensignsoftware.com

eSignal (also operates QCharts)—www.esignal.com

TradeStation—www.tradestation.com

TRADING-RELATED WEB SITES

www.brettsteenbarger.com

www.cboe.com

www.cbot.com

www.cme.com

www.ensignsoftware.com/help/simbroker.htm—Simulated Trading

www.markdouglas.com

www.tradingliveonline.com

www.tradingtutor.com

Index

A

AB=CD pattern:
  CD leg variations, 43–46
  characteristics of, 42
  description of, 39
  history of, 37–38
  psychology of, 48
  slope and time frames of, 46–47
  structure of, 39–41
  trading, 49–52
  on trend day, 135–136, 137
Adams, Evangeline, 12
Alcoa (AA), 103–104
Allen, James, 188
As a Man Thinketh (Allen), 188
Asymmetrical geometric pattern,
    9–10
At-the-money call option, 162

B

Barrick Gold Corporation (ABX), 83
Bayer, George, 9, 11
Broadening Top and Bottom patterns:
  adding Fibonacci ratios to, 127–128
  failure point on, 129
  identification of, 126–127
  structure of, 126–127
  trading, 129–130

Burrell, Lisa, 11
Business plan, annual, 176–177
Butterfly pattern:
  characteristics of, 71–72
  description of, 69–70
  history of, 67–68
  psychology of, 72–73
  structure of, 70–71
  trading, 73–80
Buy and sell, 40, 56, 68
Buy or sell orders, entering incorrect,
    179

C

Call options, 161, 162, 165–166
Casinos, 150–151
CD leg phenomena variations, 43–46
Centex Corporation (CTX), 100, 101
Classical technical analysis patterns,
    113
Cole, George, 114
Computer crashes, 179
Confirmation signs, in trade
    management, 152–154
Conti Commodity Trading, 20
Contracts, calculating number of,
    158–159
Corn, 110, 129

Countertrend trades, managing, 118–119
Crabel, Toby, 134
Crawford, Arch, 12
The Crawford Perspectives, 12
Crude oil:
  Butterfly sell pattern, 77–79
  Double Top pattern, 119, 120
  futures of, 19, 20
  harmonic numbers, 34

D
Daily routine of traders. *See also* Traders
  mental preparation, 187–188
  physical preparation, 188–189
  trade preparation, 183–186
Day Trading with Short Term Price Patterns and Opening Range Breakout (Crabel), 134
Disaster plans, 177–181
Distractions, traders and, 180
Double Bottom pattern:
  characteristics of, 115–116
  example of, 116–117
  failure point on, 120
  recognizing, 119
  trend clues of, 117–119
Double Top pattern:
  characteristics of, 115–116
  example of, 119, 120
  failure point on, 120
  recognizing, 119–120
Douglas, Mark, 151, 170, 171, 187
Dow, Charles, 114
Dow futures, 20, 21, 24–26
Dow Index, 116, 117–119, 128

Dow Jones Industrial Average, 34, 116, 127
Downtrend, 21

E
The Egg of Columbus (Bayer), 11
Elliott, Ralph, 114
Elliott, W. D., 69
EOG Resources (EOG), 44
Equal time phenomenon, 117
Euro currency, 29–30, 45
Euro futures, 78–79
Euro with Gartley "222" sell pattern, 108–109
Expanding Triangle pattern, 128

F
Failure point:
  Broadening Top and Bottom patterns, 129–130
  Double Bottom pattern, 121
  Double Top pattern, 120
  Head and Shoulders Bottom pattern, 125
  Head and Shoulders Top pattern, 123
Fibonacci ratios:
  adding to Broadening Top and Bottom patterns, 128–129
  applying, 15–18
  applying to Head and Shoulders Top pattern, 122
  combining with harmonic numbers in S&P 500 E-mini, 32
  for moving stop-loss order, 119
  origin and principles of, 11–15
  patterns, 9–13
  on trend days, 138–140

Fibonacci retracement pattern, 92–99

Fibonacci retracement ratio, 55, 58

Fibonacci retracement setups, 106–109

Fibonacci tools, software with, 194

The Frank Tubbs Stock Market Course (Tubbs), 38

G

Gann, W. D., 9, 11, 20, 68, 93, 114, 117

Garrett, William, 12

Gartley, H. M., 37, 39, 51–53, 114, 127

Gartley "222" pattern:
   characteristics of, 57–59
   description of, 55–56
   history of, 53–55
   psychology of, 59–60
   sell pattern, 158–159
   structure of, 56–57
   trading, 60–66

Geometric patterns, 9–18

The Geometry of Markets (Gann, Bayer, Gilmore), 9

Gilmore, Bryce, 9, 67

Golden mean ratio, 13–14

Gold futures, 23–24, 89, 90, 95

Goldman Sachs (GS), 101–103

Gold market, harmonic numbers in, 34

Google (GOOG):
   Butterfly pattern, 105, 106
   Gartley "222" pattern, 63–66, 69
   micro view of trade entry, 107
   repetitive swings formation, 26, 27
   time in symmetry of patterns, 45

Grant, Kenneth L., 150

H

Harmonic numbers:
   defined, 20
   finding, 28–30
   origin of, 19–20
   in other markets, 34
   repetition in price swings, 24–28
   in S&P 500, 30–31, 32
   using expansions of, 30, 33
   using 3 percent rule for, 33–34
   vibrations in price swings, 21–24

Head and Shoulders Bottom pattern, 123–125, 126

Head and Shoulders pattern, 121–123

Head and Shoulders Top pattern, 122, 123, 125

Hill, Napoleon, 188

I

IBM:
   harmonic swings forming AB=CD pattern, 37
   Head and Shoulder Top pattern, 124, 125
   Head and Shoulder Top pattern with Fibonacci ratios application, 122
   using harmonic numbers for stop-loss orders, 33, 34

Intel (INTC), 46, 95–96, 152, 153

In-the-money call option, 162

L

Liber abaci (Book of Calculation) (Leonardo), 13–14

Light from Many Lamps (Watson), 188

"Lighting bolt" shape, of buy and sell patterns, 40
Lindsey, Charles, 38

M
MacKay, Peggy, 99
Market(s):
    harmonic numbers in, 34
    history of geometry in, 11–12
    premaket trade preparation, 184
    preparation after market hours, 185–186
    preparation during market hours, 184–185
    setup for opening price Retracement trade, 99–100
    vibrations in, 20, 21–24, 28
Market Wizards (Schwager), 114
Merck, 39, 41
Microsoft (MSFT), 162, 163
Money management, 149–160
Morgan, J. Pierpont, 11
Multiple time frames:
    advantages of, 104–106
    managing risk using, 106–108
    multiple pattern completion, 108–111
    opposing patterns on, 109–111

N
Narrowing of range (NR7), 134
NASDAQ-100 (QQQQ), 86–87, 96–98, 154
News announcements/exchange closures, unexpected, 180–181

O
Opening Price Principle (Pesavento and Mackay), 99
Opening Price Retracement patterns, 99–100
Opening Price Retracement setups, 99, 101–104
Opening Price Retracement trade, market setup for, 99–100
Options:
    controlling risk with, 163–164
    with extension patterns, 164–167
    factors influencing price of, 162–165
    utilizing call and put options, 164
Order entry errors, 180
Out-of-the money call /put option, 162, 165

P
Parallel trend lines, 38
Performance, tracking, 172
Pesavento, Larry, 55, 99
Pfizer Butterfly buy pattern, 73–77
Physical preparation of traders, 189–190
Power outages, 180
Premarket trade preparation, 184
Price swings, 21, 23–24, 24–28
Price symmetry, in three drive pattern, 84
Profits in the Stock Market (Gartley), 39, 53–55, 127
Put option, 161–162, 164–165

R

Range, 20, 31, 32, 134
Raschke, Linda, 134
Repetition, 20, 24–28
Research in Motion Limited (RIMM), 94
Resources for traders, 191–194
Reverse Point Wave system, 127
Risk, 155–160, 163–164

S

Sandisk Corporation, 157
Schabacker, R. W., 113, 114, 115, 124, 126
Schwager, Jack, 114
Schwartz, Marty, 114
Sideways-trading market, 20, 21
Silver market, harmonic numbers in, 34
Soybeans:, 34, 61–63, 71, 163–164
S&P 500. *See also* S&P 500 E-mini
   harmonic numbers in, 30–31, 32
   put option purchase, 164–165
   on September 11, 2001, 179
   tweezer top and bottom pattern, 59
S&P 500 E-mini
   AB=CD buy and sell patterns, 40
   extension of CD leg, 47
   Fibonacci Retracement pattern, 93
   5-minute hand chart, 187
   Gartley "222" pattern, 65–66, 158–159, 168–169
   harmonic swings forming, 26, 27
   price in trend form, 23
   retracement pattern, 93, 98–99

three drives pattern, 87–90
trading AB=CD pattern, 49–51
trading trend day, 132–134, 141–144
trend day, 145–146
Stock Market Theory and Practice (Schabacker), 113, 124, 126
Stop-loss orders, 33
Strike price, 162–163
Swings, 20
Symmetrical geometric pattern, 10, 13
Symmetry, in Butterfly pattern, 72

T

Technical analysis:
   basics of, 115
   Broadening Top and Bottom patterns, 126–130
   double bottom and top patterns, 115–121
   head and shoulders pattern, 120–126
   history of, 114–115
Think and Grow Rich (Hill), 188
Three drives pattern:
   characteristics of, 84–85
   description of, 82–83
   history of, 81–82
   psychology of, 85
   structure of, 83–84
   trading, 85–90
   3 percent rule, in harmonic numbers, 33–34
Thrust, in Butterfly pattern, 72
Time symmetry, 84, 122

Torque Analysis of Stock Market Cycles (Garrett), 12

Total Trading capital, using percentage of, 155–160

Trade management. *See also* Trading
confirmation signs, 153–155
steps of, 149–150
thinking in probabilities, 150–151
warning signs, 152

Traders. *See also* Daily routine of traders
reasons for failure, 6–7
reasons for success, 5–6
resources for, 191–194
thinking in probabilities, 150
using performance statistics, 172–174

Trades Worksheet, twenty sample, 171

Trade tracking sheet, 186

Trading. *See also* Trade management; Trading plan
AB=CD pattern, 49–52
Broadening Top and Bottom patterns, 130
Butterfly pattern, 73–81
Gartley "222" pattern, 60–66
Head and Shoulders Top pattern, 123
mistakes in, 160
Opening Price Retracement setups, 101–104
from short time frame, 133
successful, steps for, 5–6
three drives pattern, 85–90
trend day, 141–146

Trading in the Zone (Douglas), 151, 170, 171, 188

Trading plan. *See also* Money management
annual business plan, 176–177
benefits of, 167–168
daily, 168–174
disaster plans, 177–181
software, computer, and office costs, 176
tracking performance, 172
trading as a business, 174–176
using trader performance statistics, 172–174

Trading Risk: Enhanced Profitability through Risk Control (Grant), 150

Trend, 20, 131, 132

Trend day consolidation pattern, 136–138

Trend days
controlling risk on, 140–142
Fibonacci ratios on, 138–140, 141
identifying, 132–133
patterns on, 135–138
trading, 141–146

Trident: A Trading Strategy (Lindsay), 38

Tubbs, Frank, 38

Tweezer bottoms, 58, 153–154

Tweezer top, 58

Twentyman, Jim, 19–20

U

Uptrend, example of, 20, 22

W

Wal-Mart (WMT), 51–52
Warning signs, in trade management,
    152
Watson, Lillian, 188
Waver Trader Program, 67,
    68

W bottoms. *See* Double Bottom
    Pattern; Double Top pattern
Westinghouse Electric, 124
Wetzel, A. W., 126
Wheat, 28, 35
Wilder, J. Welles, 127
Wyckoff, Richard, 114